P-38 LIGHTNING

in action

by Gene B Stafford

illustrated by Don Greer

P-38 LIGHTNING
in action

squadron/signal publications
AIRCRAFT NO. 25
$3.95

[Cover] "Haleakala", piloted by H.H. "Lighthorse Harry" Sealy. Flying with the 459th Fighter Squadron out of Chittagong, India.

 squadron/signal publications

A brand new P-38L-1-LO banks over the southern California countryside. The standard factory markings applied to the ship show up well in this shot. [W. Hess]

Photo Credits
US Air Force
US AF Museum
80th Fighter Squadron Assoc.
479th Fighter Group

S. Woods	D. Glover
J. Loisel	D. Morris
H. Brown	R. Dillon
R. Anderson	W. Jordan
H. Hatch	W. Hess
W. Broadfoot	L. Carr
D. Robinson	J. McClure
R. Smith	W. Thompson
W. Smelzer	O. Taylor
E. Geiger	H. Crim
R. Englehart	

Also by Gene Stafford
Thunderbolt in Action
by Gene Stafford & William Hess
Aces of the Eighth

COLOR KEY

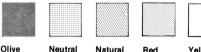

Olive Drab	Neutral Grey	Natural Metal	Red	Yellow

White	Black	Medium Blue	Insignia Blue	Bright Green

NOTE: WHERE SQUADRON COLOR IS INDICATED THE BASIC DESIGN REMAINED THE SAME. JUST THE SQUADRON COLOR CHANGED.

The clean lines that marked the XP-38 were carried through on subsequent production versions. Aside from relatively minor changes, the basic plane that rolled off the assembly lines in 1945 was quite similar to the first ship. [80th Fighter Squadron Association]

With only a few hours of flying time under its belt, the XP-38 was flown on a cross-country mission from the West Coast to the East Coast in just under eight hours. Though the plane crashed at the end of the flight, the army had seen enough to convince it that the big ship was worth putting in production. [Air Force Museum]

The Star is Born

In 1926, the fledgling Lockheed Aircraft Company, under the direction of Malcolm and Allen Lockheed and John Northrop, introduced the first high performance business plane - the Vega. Other ships such as the Sirius, Altair and Orion soon followed. Until the crash of the stock market in 1929 things looked bright for the young company, but from that point on, the outlook was much less clear. By 1932, it appeared the company would follow many others into bankruptcy; but such was not to be. Robert Gross, Carl Squier and Lloyd Stearman believed the company had a future and went to the U.S. District Court in Los Angeles where they purchased Lockheed for the princely sum of $40,000.

The first new design to come from the reorganized company was the twin-engined Electra. In March 1933, a model of this new ship was sent to the University of Michigan for wind tunnel tests. One of the men responsible for the tests was a young engineer by the name of Clarence L. "Kelly" Johnson. The Lockheed management was so impressed with Johnson that he was hired. This proved an extremely wise move, for four years later, the design of the P-38 would spring from his fertile mind.

By 1936, the Army Air Corps was well aware of fighter developments in Europe. Though most of the American effort was devoted to bomber aircraft, a general specification was issued in 1936 for a high altitude interceptor. These specifications called for an aircraft with a speed of 360 mph at 20,000 feet and

an endurance of one hour at full throttle. Though Lockheed had never built a fighter, the decision was made to go after this one.

Kelly Johnson, the man given the responsibility at Lockheed for the design of the new fighter, realized a radical departure from present pursuit standards was necessary to meet the performance goals. Allison had an engine, the V-1710, that fit the needs of the new ship but only if two were used. Several concepts were considered, but the one final selection was an aircraft with the pilot located in a central nacelle and two booms, containing the superchargers, carrying through to the tail. The armament selected was unusually heavy for the period and comprised four 23 millimeter cannon and four .50 caliber machine guns mounted in the nose. Another innovation included in the design was a tricycle landing gear.

A proposal based on the new design, now called the Lockheed Model 22, was submitted to Wright Field for consideration. The performance detailed in the proposal exceeded that required in the original specification. The Model 22 would have a top speed of 417 mph at 20,000 feet, a climb rate sufficient to reach this altitude in four and a half minutes and an endurance of 105 minutes at 393 mph. After reviewing the proposal, the Army issued a contract to Lockheed for a single aircraft, the XP-38, on 23 June 1937. The value of the contract was $163,000.

When Lockheed won the XP-38 contract, it had some 2,500 employees and these were of the old school where pride of accomplishment was important. The men assigned to the XP-38 lavished considerable attention on the big fighter. The ship was practically hand-built, and the excellent workmanship showed when the plane was rolled out for the first time. Every inch of it was polished to a high gloss.

The pilot of the cross-country flight was Ben Kelsey. He is shown here during his brief stop-over at Wright Field, Ohio. [Air Force Museum]

The XP-38 was shipped by truck to nearby March Field for tests, but these had hardly begun when problems began to appear. During the initial taxi trials, the brakes failed and the shiny new plane ran into a ditch. Fortunately, the damage was slight and tests were soon resumed. On 27 January 1939, Lt. Ben

Kelsey readied the ship for its first flight. Shortly after the plane became airborne, a part in the Fowler-flap failed and created a drastic change to the aerodynamic characteristics of the ship. Kelsey was an experienced test pilot and was able to bring the XP-38 under control. To everyone's relief, he brought the plane in and landed without any further damage.

The Army Air Corps was very publicity conscious during the Thirties. What it lacked in quantity, it made up for in words and eye-catching demonstrations. Even so, it was a little surprising when it was announced that the XP-38 would be used to make a high speed flight across the country. Here was an aircraft, one of a kind, with only six hours of flight time under its belt; and one that had experienced small but vexing problems from the beginning. Ben Kelsey was named to pilot the plane on the flight from March Field to Wright Field (and on to Mitchell Field if things went well) with an intermediate stop at Amarillo, Texas for fuel.

Sunrise was still several hours away when Kelsey climbed into the cockpit of the XP-38 to complete his pre-flight check on 11 February 1939. With everything in order, he hit the starter and the big Allison engines roared to life. Kelsey taxied to the end of the runway and, with a last glance at all the instruments, started to roll down the runway. At 80 mph, the big ship lifted clear of the ground and headed toward Amarillo. The official take off time was noted as 0912 (EST).

No problems developed on the first two legs of the flight. Kelsey stopped only long enough to take on fuel at Texas and Wright Field and headed for Mitchell Field. Arriving over Mitchell Field at 1655 EST, Kelsey made one pass over the base at an altitude of 1,000 feet, but as he turned to make his landing, problems developed. The young test pilot saw a line of trees ahead of him and tried to add power to raise the plane over them. The right engine failed to respond so Kelsey cut back power on the good engine to avoid a low altitude spin. The lowered landing gear caught the uppermost branches of the trees, and the big fighter plane slammed to the ground in a sand trap on the local golf course. The time was 1657, but the end of the mission was not what had been expected.

Kelsey climbed from the cockpit with nothing hurt except his pride. He had flown 2490 miles with an elapsed time of just seven hours and 43 minutes. Only Howard Hughes had bettered this time in a specially equipped plane on a non-stop flight. The XP-38 had demonstrated to the world that the United States at last had a world class fighter.

The Army was more interested in performance than in the fact that the XP-38 had crashed. As a result, it viewed with favor a proposal submitted by Lockheed just two days after the crash. In one sense, the loss of the XP-38 may have been a blessing. If the plane had not been lost, tests would have been continued for some time and the order for new ships may have been delayed by several months - a period the United States could ill afford. Because of loss, the Air Corps gave Lockheed a contract on 27 April in the amount of $2,180,728 to deliver thirteen service test fighters. These ships were to be designated YP-38.

The YP-38 was similar to the X-model, but there were numerous changes made in the design. A pair of radiators were now carried in each boom, rather than the single one in the XP-38. The rotation of the props was changed and armament was reduced to a single 37 millimeter cannon, two .30 caliber machine guns and two .50 caliber guns. The greatest effort to be expended,

In October 1939, the Army let a contract to Lockheed for a new version of the P-38. This ship, designated the XP-49, differed from the earlier ship primarily in the engine. Though the XP-49 did fly for the first time in November 1942, it never entered production. The performance was not significantly better than the P-38 to warrant changing the production lines. [W. Hess]

Though it bore a resemblence to the P-38, the XP-58 was a brand new and larger airplane. The ship was begun in 1940 but it was June 1944 before it flew for the first time. In part, a victim of changing priorities, the ship never was ordered into production. [80th Fighter Squadron Association]

however, was in a weight reduction program and a redesign to make the ship ready for production rather than hand assembly. Altogether, some 30,000 drawing changes were made.

The first YP-38, serial number 39-689, was rolled out in early September 1940. On the 16th of the month, Marshall Headle took the ship up on its maiden flight. For more than the next year, the various service test Lightnings were subjected to exhaustive tests to explore the performance envelope completely. Numerous problems arose but the two most critical were buffeting and compressibility. The former was solved by adding closely fitted fillets to the wing roots. The problem with compressibility, however, would take several years to solve. This problem would claim the life of Ralph Virden in November 1941, but it did not stop the development of the fighter.

The outbreak of war in Europe in September 1939 put the United States in a position where something had to be done to modernize the fighter strength of the AAC. As a result, the time between each phase of fighter development was cut or eliminated. On 16 September 1939, the Army Air Corps placed an order with Lockheed for 66 aircraft of which the first eighteen were to be P-38s and the remainder P-38Ds. The XP-38A was actually the nineteenth ship in the production order and it was completed to test use of a pressurized cabin. The designations P-38B and C were not used. Aside from aerodynamic refinements and the addition of self-sealing fuel tanks, the P-38D differed little from the service test models. Armament had, however, been changed again - this time to four .50 caliber machine guns as companion pieces to the 37 millimeter cannon.

Though the P-38D was a step in the right direction, it was still not classed as a combat ready airplane. The first true combat version of the Lightning was the E-model. In August 1940, still a month before the first flight of the YP-38, the Air Corps placed an order with Lockheed for 210 of this variant and a further order for 75 P-38Fs. The 37mm cannon of the earlier models gave way to the more reliable 20mm cannon. This, plus interior design changes, allowed almost double the ammunition load to be carried. Other changes included bullet-proof fuel tanks, an oxygen system for the pilot and armor plate protection for him. The F-model saw a change to the Allison V-1710-F5 engine, and provision was made for carrying two 150 gallon fuel tanks externally beneath the inner wing panels. In addition to the 75 P-38Fs ordered in August, the AAC ordered an additional 195 ships on the same day Marshall Headle flew the YP-38 for the first time. At this point, Lockheed had orders for some 500 Lightnings. The company's future in the fighter business was assured.

Following the F-model (a total of 527 aircraft built) on the Lockheed production lines were the P-38G (1,082 aircraft) and H (601 aircraft built). These variants were virtually identical externally with the earlier models. Later versions of the Allison engine were the major change, but the underwing racks were strengthened to increase fuel or bomb load. With this modification, the P-38G had a combat range of just over 2,000 miles.

The major external change to the Lightning came with the introduction of the P-38J. The carburetor air intercoolers were moved from the leading edge of the wing to the forward part of the engine nacelles - giving the plane the characteristic chin seen on all subsequent aircraft. The curved windscreen of the earlier ships was replaced by one with an optically flat surface. This gave the pilot greater protection and also better vision. The late J-models and the L-models had another important addition. A dive flap was added beneath the main spar to provide a nose-up moment when the plane went into a dive. With this change, the problem with compressibility was finally solved. Hydraulic boost was added to the ailerons, a change that greatly improved the roll rate of the big fighter. Additional underwing strong points were used on the P-38L for rockets. In all, 2,970 P-38Js and 3,923 P-38Ls were built. The latter included some 113 aircraft build by Consolidated Vultee in Nashville, Tennessee.

[Right] Pilot's cockpit detail in the P-38M. [W. Thompson]

[Below Right] The radar operator's cockpit in the P-38M. The radar scope is the tubular device near the top of the windscreen. [W. Thompson]

Interior shop of an early Lightning. Later versions were similar but among the major visible changes was a flat rather than a rounded windscreen. [Air Force Museum]

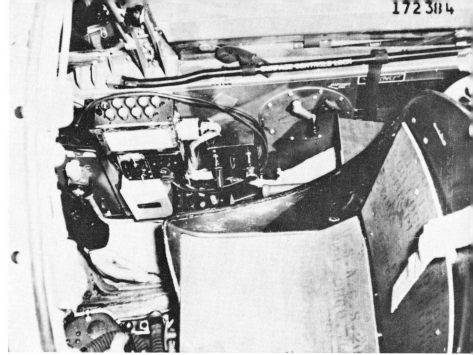

LOCKHEED P-38L

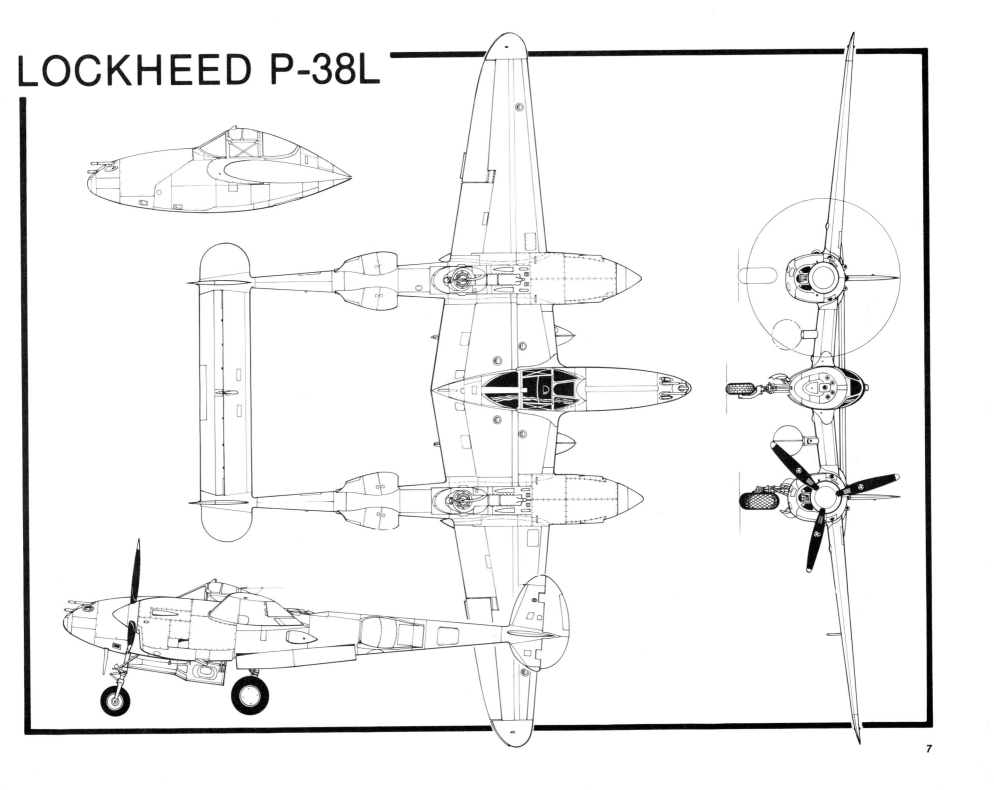

Development

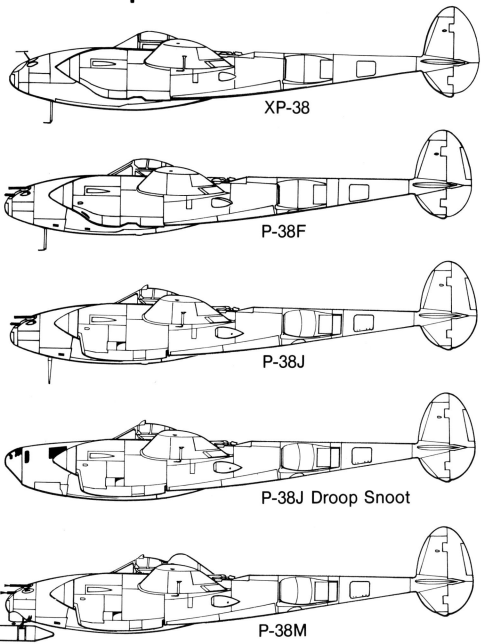

XP-38

P-38F

P-38J

P-38J Droop Snoot

P-38M

To meet the needs for a speedy night fighter, several P-38Ls were modified as the two-place P-38M. This ship carried all the normal armament but, in addition, a spare seat for a radar operator and radar sets were carried. [W. Thompson]

The business end of the "Night Lightning". The guns had special blast shields on the muzzles to prevent blinding of the pilot when the guns were fired. The radar system used was the AN/APS-4. [W. Thompson]

The British ordered an aircraft similar to the P-38E under the designation the Model 322. For some reason the British ordered the ship without superchargers and with props that rotated in the same direction. As a result, the tests on the two ships delivered to England were not impressive and the remainder of the order for 143 planes was cancelled. [80th Fighter Sq.]

The remainder of the Model 322s completed by Lockheed were sent to Dallas, Texas for modification. Subsequently, the ships were used as trainers and other odd jobs under the designation: P-322. [L. Carr]

Into Service

In August 1941, the last of the P-38Ds was completed followed in October by the first of the combat ready E-model. As the USAAF took delivery of these ships, they were quickly assigned to the rapidly expanding number of fighter groups. The first unit to take the new fighter on strength was, appropriately enough, the 1st Fighter Group. This outfit was an old line unit with its roots in World War I. Other groups such as the 14th, 82nd, 56th, 55th and 78th also were assigned the Lightning in the days following America's entry into the war.

Though no P-38s were involved in the attack on Pearl Harbor or the events occuring shortly thereafter, Lightning equipped units were transferred to the West Coast to provide protection in case Japanese raids were launched. Along with patrols, these units developed the skills and techniques they would need later. One group thus involved was the 55th Fighter Group, based at Paine Field, Washington. The 54th Fighter Squadron of this group was sent on detached service to Alaska and the 11th Air Force. The 11th had been formed in February 1942 to protect the Aleutians and Alaska from enemy attacks. Upon arrival in the far north, the 54th was assigned to the one fighter group in residence - the 343rd. One month later, the Japanese invaded the Aleutians.

The air war in the far north was on a small scale in terms of the number of men and aircraft involved but it was a particularly vicious one for the pilots.

Weather was extremely poor much of the time, and a pilot forced down in the cold arctic waters had very little chance for survival. Most of the missions for the P-38s were routine patrols with no enemy contact. Ironically, however, the first blood for the Lightning was drawn over American territory in this least known of the battlefields where it would fight, when Lieutenants Stanley Long and Kenneth Ambrose shot down two Mavis flying-boats near Adak, Alaska on August 4, 1942.

At a formal dinner in Washington in March 1942, a member of Roosevelt's Cabinet leaned over to his dinner partner and asked: "With shipping as scarce as it is, how can we get more fighters to England." The man to whom the question was asked answered, with a slight touch of humor in his voice: "I guess we'll just have to fly them there."

Two days later, President Roosevelt placed a phone call to the second man at the dinner and asked if he really did think American fighters could be flown across the Atlantic. Roosevelt could hardly have directed the question to a better person, for he was General H.H. "Hap" Arnold. Though he didn't know for certain, Arnold did believe such a thing was in the realm of possibility. After all, bombers and transports were already making this flight on a routine basis. Also, work had begun on bases in Labrador and Greenland, and these would soon be available. The fighters, could, therefore, make the journey in a series of hops. After deliberation, it was decided to make the flight, and Brigadier Generals Carl Spaatz and Frank Hunter were given the job of planning the mission.

To see whether the Lightning could be used on skis, a P-38J-1-L0 was converted to test the installation. The results of the test showed the conversion was possible but not practical. [Air Force Museum]

Among the States side units to equip with the P-38 was the 56th Fighter Group. John McClure poses for his picture in a ship taken on strength by the 62nd Squadron. Shortly after this the group converted to the P-47. [J. McClure]

The original plan developed by Spaatz and Hunter called for two P-38 groups (1st and 4th) and one P-39 group (52nd) to make the flight in the company of a B-17 group. The latter would provide the navigation for the fighters. The 320 fighters would proceed from Presque Isle, Maine, to Goose Bay, Labrador, then on to Greenland, Iceland and finally into the United Kingdom. On paper, the mission looked like a simple cross-country flight with several hops; but this was not the case. Vast stretches of uncharted ice and frozen sea lay between each stop. Vagaries in weather were also common; and there was little in the way of weather forecasting in the remote areas to be covered. In addition, the aircraft had to be fitted with special radio gear, improved oxygen systems and long range fuel tanks.

The first flight of Lightnings left Presque Isle for Goose Bay on 27 June and by 6 July the entire complement of 1st Fighter Group ships had made the first two hops successfully. Weather did cause a few anxious moments for several of the pilots when they ran into an unexpected fog on the way into Greenland. The fighters became separated from their lead ship and had to come in using their own navigational ability.

The flight from Greenland to Iceland was the most dangerous part of the mission. Not only did the ships have to fly across the wasteland of central Greenland, but they also had to fly across a large stretch of ocean - one where shipping was sparse. The only aircraft lost by the 1st came during this segment. Six P-38s and a single B-17 lead ship were several hours out from home when fog was encountered. The men decided to return but weather back at base was closing in rapidly and a landing would be impossible by the time the seven planes arrived. There was no choice but to go on. Five hours into the mission, the pilots were still in the soup so a turn to the south was made so they would remain over land.

After nine hours in the air, the planes were practically running on fumes. Joseph McManus led the ships down to scout the terrain below. The young flight leader then went even lower to see if a landing could be made on what appeared to be a rather smooth area. With his gear down, he swept in, but as he started to climb back, both engines quit and he was forced to land. The nose wheel hit a fissure and McManus injured his shoulder in the process. The other pilots knew their fuel would also be exhausted in the very near future, so they decided to land and share a common fate with McManus. One by one, the P-38s and then the B-17 set down. No further injuries occured, but there was still a major hurdle - the men had to survive. Five days later, the men were located and all flown back to base.

By 27 July, two squadrons of the 1st had completed the journey to Prestwick, Scotland. Though six P-38s had been lost, all of the men were safe. The group had given proof to Hap Arnold's belief that fighters could be ferried across the Atlantic. Others would follow but the pilots were proud of the fact that they had been first.

The third squadron of the group (the 27th) took a little longer to reach the United Kingdom. The squadron had been the first to reach Iceland so it was detailed to provide air defense as the other aircraft came through. In this role, the 27th joined the P-40-equipped 33rd Fighter Squadron. For most of the stay, the duty tended to boredom. Every once in a while, a scramble would be called to try and intercept the FW-200s of KG/40 as the big ships flew near Iceland on maritime patrol. Usually these came to naught, but on 15 August, Lt. Elza Shahan destroyed a Condor over Iceland, scoring the first P-38 victory against the Luftwaffe.

The fighter groups arriving from the United States were assigned to the 8th Air Force. At the time, this organization was being used as a foundation for building the combat readiness of the units slated for the North African invasion. The strategic might of the 8th, the overwhelming armada of bombers charged with bringing Germany to its knees, would have to wait almost a year before it would be a reality. Though the 1st, 14th, and 82nd Fighter Groups were assigned to the 8th initially, all three would go on to Africa.

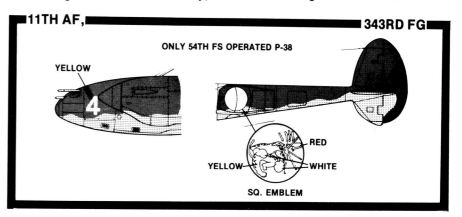

11TH AF, 343RD FG

ONLY 54TH FS OPERATED P-38

YELLOW

RED

YELLOW — — WHITE

SQ. EMBLEM

On one mission, a 14th Fighter Group pilot got into a literal scrape with a Bf 109. The German plane slid back along the inside of the right boom and almost totally severed the horizontal tail. The American pilot flew home with his ship in this condition. He was ordered to bail out rather than try to land. [O. Taylor]

Another 14th Group pilot had his engine shot out and came home. When he tried to land, he found the gear wouldn't come down and he was forced to bring it in on its belly. It was events such as these two that made the Lightning extremely popular with the pilots. [H. Crim]

The 5,000th Lightning built was painted a brilliant vermillion. The plane, a P-38J-20-Lo carried the name "YIPPEE" in large letters under the wings as well as on the nose. [W. Hess]

Harley Vaughn beside the nose of his ship. Vaughn was a seven victory ace with the 82nd Group. [W. Jorda]

Above the Mediterranean

The culmination of several months of detailed planning came on 8 November 1942 with the opening of Operation Torch - the Allied invasion of northwest Africa. American troops, followed by British forces, poured ashore at Algiers, Oran and Casablanca against light or no resistance. The initial objectives of the invasion were attained with the surrender of Algeria and Morocco two days after the landings, but the objective of capturing Tunis eluded the Allies. In the race for this all-important port city, the Germans won and stopped the American and British troops in a battle before the city. What had been hoped would be a short campaign settled into a prolonged and bloody struggle.

Morocco and Algeria had fallen before the P-38Fs of the 1st Fighter group arrived on the scene. The ground personnel of the group, however, had been among the troops wading ashore on 8 November. On 13 November 1942, the Lightnings took off from their base in England and, after a flight of several hours, arrived at the new home for the unit - Tafaraoui, near Oran. On the 15th, two squadrons of the 14th Fighter Group winged their way along the same course to bring the strength of the Lockheed fighter to five squadrons.

The enemy facing the 1st and 14th was well seasoned and experienced. In particular, the Luftwaffe elements in Africa had good aircraft and over three years of experience in aerial warfare. The first several months of action by the Twelfth Air Force was a period of extremely vicious and bloody action. Though actions were often on a small scale in terms of the number of aircraft involved, this did nothing to lessen its intensity.

One early mission flown by the 49th Fighter Squadron (14th Fighter Group) was an escort for A-20s to Bizerte. One flight flew close to the bombers while two others flew looser escort. The formation was attacked by a gaggle of Bf 109s which were engaged by the two outlying flights of P-38s. In the ensuing fight, five of the German ships were knocked down, but the Americans lost a similar number. Russell Gustke, one of the pilots on the mission had these comments: "Had the two flights been able to stay together, concentrating on warding off the enemy attack, they all would have returned home. Another flight probably could have helped our aircraft by giving them a brief relief during which time they could have reorganized themselves." Through such post-flight comments, P-38 tactics slowly evolved, but it was a difficult process.

A third P-38 outfit, the 82nd Fighter Group, followed the two original units to Africa in late December 1942 and settled in at Telergma. On the flight from England, the 80 planes encountered two Ju 88s over the Bay of Biscay and downed them both. The 82nd, therefore, had the distinction of scoring its first victories even before it flew its first official combat mission.

The pilots of the 82nd arrived to what they thought was an extremely warm reception in North Africa. The 1st and 14th had suffered heavily in the month and a half of combat before the arrival of the new group, and the veteran pilots of these units viewed the 80 new Lightnings as a fine replacement pool. No sooner did an 82nd pilot step down from his plane than one from the 1st or 14th would hop in and roar off to his own base. Before the new arrivals realized what was going on, the group found itself with less than half the planes it was authorized. With new aircraft deliveries from the States being slow, it was some two months before the 82nd was up to full strength. In the interim, the pilots took turns flying the ships that were available.

When the 14th arrived in North Africa, there were only two squadrons assigned to it. The third squadron remained behind in Iceland to provide air defense for that island. Between its first mission (18 November 1942) and 23 January, the group's 48th Fighter Squadron lost a total of thirteen pilots and some twenty aircraft. This was equivalent to half the authorized pilot strength and virtually the entire complement of Lightnings with which the squadron entered combat. Losses in both categories had been replaced but not to the extent of the losses. On the mission of 23 January, the squadron lost five pilots. For a group that had entered combat well under strength, these losses were simply too great. The fact that the pilots had shot down more planes than they had lost was of little consolation. The pilots refused to fly further missions.

There were serious discussions about completely striking the 14th from the USAAF roles because it had disgraced itself in combat. This was not the case, and cooler heads prevailed. Flying personnel were reassigned, but the ground organization was kept together. The group was pulled from combat to refit and rest. During this period, a third fighter squadron was assigned to the group (the 37th). At the end of the refit, the 14th went back on full combat operations with a full complement of men and machines.

As winter progressed and turned to spring, the tide of the aerial battle in North African began to shift in favor of the Allies. The tactics developed in the dark early days of the campaign had been polished to the point where the men who flew had confidence in themselves and their aircraft. A major factor in the success was the arrival of new machines and men in ever-increasing numbers for the Allied forces. The Axis forces, however, saw a down turn in their resupply. With the British and Americans in control of the sea, the Germans tried to bring in supplies by air. Once air superiority was lost, this became an almost impossible task and the final result in Africa could only be postponed - not avoided.

On 5 April 1943, 32 Lightnings of the 82nd Fighter Group took off from Berteaux to escort B-25s on a sweep. Some fifteen miles north of Cap Bon, an enemy convoy of six to ten ships was sighted. The Mitchells went down to attack while the P-38s circled above. While this action was in progress, a large formation of German aircraft was spotted. Like a swarm of angry bees, the Lightnings headed for the lumbering Ju 52s and their escort of Bf 109s, Bf 110s and Ju 88s. The American fighters avoided the escort wherever possible and concentrated on the tightly packed transport formation. Airplanes were all over the sky, but the German planes continued to hold their course even though their ranks were thinned. When the battle was over, seventeen Luftwaffe aircraft had been knocked from the sky at a cost of four P-38s.

Still more evidence of the ability of the P-38 to return with battle damage was this aircraft of the 14th. Lt. Wilks brought the plane from Sardinia with one engine and his nose gear shot out. [H. Crim]

Ground crewmen of the 37th Fighter Squadron [14th Fighter Group] working on the engines. Though conditions and equipment were often poor, these men did an excellent job of keeping the planes in the air. [H. Crim]

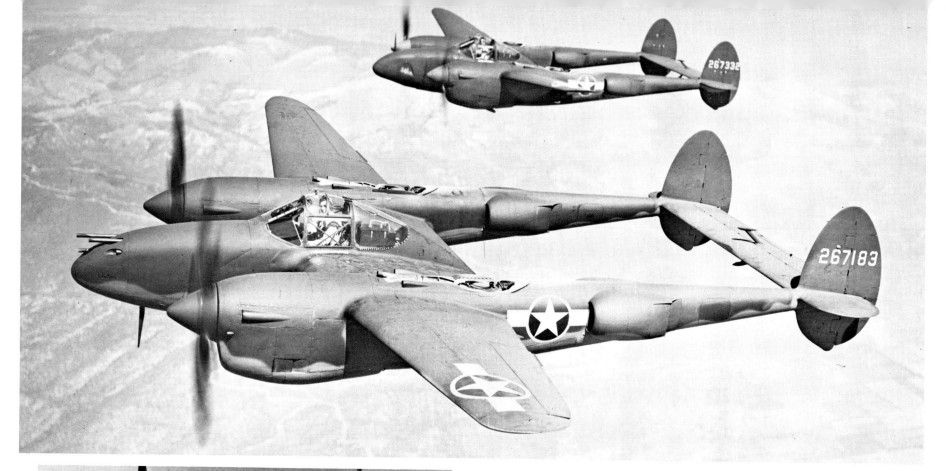

In the foreground is a P-38J-5-L0 in factory markings. For a short period during the summer of 1943, American aircraft carried the red surround to the national insignia. The ship in the background is an F-5, the photo version of the P-38. [W. Hess]

Early Marks

Canopy Development

P-38J

A formation of early P-38s over the ocean, showing to good advantage the early style supercharger and smaller air scoops.

The 1st Fighter Group also ran up a big score on the same day, when a force of 26 P-38s intercepted a formation of Ju 52s with fighter escort. Sixteen German planes were splashed including eleven of the transports. Four days later, the group ran into another Axis formation and downed 28 German planes. The inability to get supplies to the beleaguered German and Italian forces in Africa eventually caused a total collapse of resistance. On 13 May the last enemy troops in Africa stacked their arms and entered captivity.

The next step for the Allies lay across the Mediterranean Sea on the island of Sicily. Before invading this island, however, Pantelleria, an island about half way between Tunisia and Sicily, had to be neutralized. Some 10,000 enemy troops were stationed there and it could serve as a forward base for launching attacks on the invasion fleet. The decision was made to break the island with the use of air power before landing any Allied troops. Though the raids by bombers and fighters were heavy, the Allied aircraft did not meet with heavy resistance.

The invasion of Pantelleria was scheduled for 11 June, but before the troops were landed, the island surrendered. This was one of the few times in World War II when a major objective was taken strictly as a result of airpower.

Bomber and fighter raids on the next Allied objective, Sicily, were begun even before the fall of Pantelleria. The few days before the actual invasion saw an increase in tempo of the raids on Sicily. The three P-38 groups flew as many as eight missions a day against bridges, roads and fortifications on the island as part of the softening up process. These dive bombing missions continued for several days after the troops went ashore on 10 July, but once the troops were established, the Lightning pilots went back to the job of escorting the bombers on raids against Italy.

The German and Italian air forces had suffered heavy losses in Africa and the subsequent actions but there was still a large force facing the Allies in the fight above Sicily. In the five day period from 2 to 7 July Italian fighters claimed seventeen P-38s. Their own losses were also high. Two of Mussolini's top aces went down before the concentrated firepower of Lightnings in a big battle on 5 July. Capitano Franco Lucchini had 26 victories and Sottoteniente Leonardo Ferruli had 22 when they were lost.

During the last days of August and the first days of September, the 1st and 82nd Fighter Groups garnered four Distinguished Unit Citations between them. The first for each came on 25 August when the outfits participated in attacks on the complex of airfields around Foggia, Italy.

Five days later, the 1st put 48 Lightnings in the air on an escort mission to Aversa, Italy. Just after the formation of bombers and fighters crossed the enemy coast, a large force of 60 to 75 enemy aircraft attacked. The bombers continued on toward the target while the escorting P-38s engaged the attackers. Individual combats broke out all over the sky and at all altitudes from the surface of the sea on up. The attacks were well coordinated and one gaggle would attack while another reformed. The engagement lasted about forty minutes and continued for a hundred miles out to sea. Six Americans were seen to go into the sea and one collided head-on with an FW 190. Parachutes from both sides drifted down through the battle and the Mediterranean was dotted with dinghies. Eight of the German aircraft were claimed, but the cost to the 1st was high. Thirteen members of the group were listed as missing, although one pilot did show up the next day.

The 82nd won its second DUC on September 2nd under similar battle

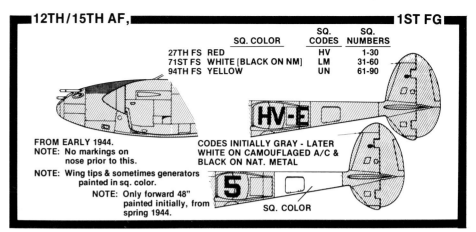

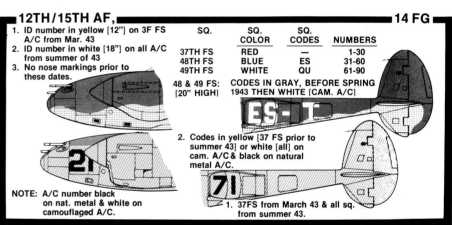

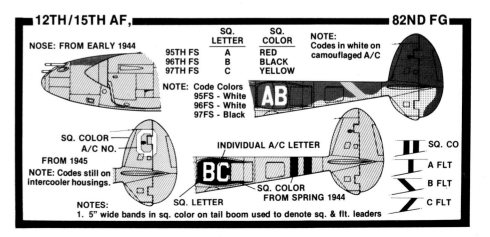

conditions. The mission was an escort to Cancello, Italy and resulted in claims for 24 German aircraft.

Winston Churchill firmly believed the fall of 1943 was an ideal time to launch a campaign in the Eastern Mediterranean to strengthen Allied-held islands and to recapture Crete. His pleas to Roosevelt, however, were rejected, but some ground, sea and air elements were sent to the area to cover operations there. The air units were the 1st and 14th Fighter Groups.

On 9 October Major William Leverette led seven P-38s of the 14th on a mission to provide top cover for elements of the British fleet. A force of some 25 to 30 Ju 87s escorted by Ju 88s was spotted heading for the ships. Leverette ordered three planes to remain as high cover while he led the others to intercept the German aircraft. In the next fifteen minutes, the Major blasted seven of the Stukas from the sky. A second pilot on the mission, Lieutenant Harry Hanna, had almost as much success by downing five enemy planes. Two days later, the 1st and 14th returned to their regular bases.

When the 37th Fighter Squadron arrived in North Africa and was assigned to the 14th Fighter Group, one of the pilots in the unit was a future ace by the name of Harry Crim. His comments on the P-38 and the air war in North Africa are of interest. "The P-38s we received in Africa were F-15LO and then, later, the H-model. This was more than likely the best production version of the Lightning ever built. The engines had been boosted to around 1800 horses and all the bugs had been worked out of the Curtiss electric props. The plane could carry 4,000 pounds of bombs and, with tanks and the cruise control techniques we worked out, it could go a long way.

"Our tactics were somewhat crude and the mission assignments limited our success of the type that made big headlines. We were fighting a first class enemy in his territory where he was fielding five aircraft to our one. Up until the invasion of Sicily, our squadron swapped about even.

"The P-38 was faster than the 109, 190 or the 202 if you had the fuel to run. The P-38 could also outclimb these three at any altitude if you used your best speed (155 indicated). The 109's best climb speed was about 120 which could cause some problems. If you climbed at his speed, he'd beat you and if you climbed at your best speed you'd over-run him. As a result, we had to learn to turn away from the 109 to outclimb him."

With the invasion of Italy and the availability of new bases for American aircraft this created, a decision was made to activate a strategic air force in the Mediterranean. The new organization, the Fifteenth Air Force, would be a companion to the Eighth then building strength in England in the attacks on the German homeland. On 3 November 1943, the Fifteenth was activated and among the units transferred to it were three P-38 groups in Africa. In December, these units moved to bases in southern Italy to begin a new chapter for themselves and the Lightning.

The 55th Fighter Group was the first to see action with the Eighth Air Force. Here a P-38H-5 of the 338th Squadron tucks its wheels after take off. The aircraft sports red surrounds to the national insignia. [80th Fighter Squadron Association]

Though the 20th Fighter Group was the first to arrive in the United Kingdom, it was not the first P-38 unit in the Eighth Air Force to enter combat. This H-5 is shown on a 20th hardstand in the fall of 1943. The three pilots use the most common mode of transportation available. [Air Force Museum]

Combat in Northern Europe

When the three P-38 groups originally assigned to the Eighth Air Force departed for North Africa in late 1942, the bomber offensive against Germany was little more than a dream. In the months that followed, however, the Eighth grew in size and expanded its scope of operations. In April 1943, three Thunderbolt equipped fighter groups went operational. These units could provide escort for the B-17 and B-24 formations as far as the occupied countries on the Continent, but Germany was well beyond fighter range. The result of not having fighter escort was graphically demonstrated on 17 August 1943 when 60 of the 325 bombers sent on the twin raids on Schweinfurt and Regensburg were lost. Long range fighters were a must.

The P-38, with its relatively long range, figured prominently in the original buildup plans of the Eighth. The 78th Fighter Group arrived in England in January 1943 with the Lightning, but shortly after this all the aircraft and most of the pilots were sent to North Africa to replace heavy losses there. The 78th never did fly the Lightning in combat and it was eight months before the next P-38 group arrived on the scene. In August, the 20th Fighter Group arrived in England followed by the 55th in September. Though both groups had worked up on the Lightning in the States, there was still much to learn before they were declared ready for combat. In addition, the flow of aircraft to the units was slowed by the demands of the Mediterranean Theater. The 55th was the

A P-38H-1 with fancy wheel covers comes in for a landing. The plane flew with the 343rd Fighter Squadron of the 55th Group. [U.S. Air Force]

ETO THEATER MARKINGS

NOSE: NONE

SQUADRON CODES

INDIVIDUAL A/C I.D.

NOTES:
1. Codes & tail symbols in white on camouflaged A/C and black on natural metal ones.
2. 24 in. tall individual A/C letter on inside of upper fin & rudder.
3. Invasion stripes painted on all operational A/C for D-Day & carried for long while after on bottom surfaces.

8TH AF, 20TH FG

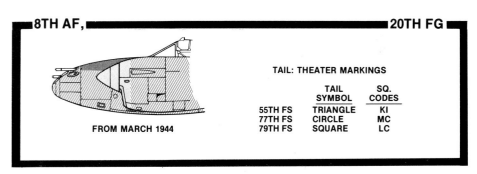

FROM MARCH 1944

TAIL: THEATER MARKINGS

	TAIL SYMBOL	SQ. CODES
55TH FS	TRIANGLE	KI
77TH FS	CIRCLE	MC
79TH FS	SQUARE	LC

8TH AF, 55TH FG

TAIL: THEATER MARKINGS

NOSE: YELLOW & WHITE CHECKER-BOARD ASSIGNED BUT NOT APPLIED

	TAIL SYMBOL	SQ. CODES
38TH FS	TRIANGLE	CG
338TH FS	CIRCLE	CL
343RD FS	SQUARE	CY

8TH AF, 364TH FG

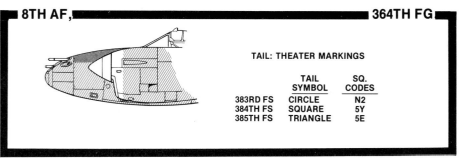

TAIL: THEATER MARKINGS

	TAIL SYMBOL	SQ. CODES
383RD FS	CIRCLE	N2
384TH FS	SQUARE	5Y
385TH FS	TRIANGLE	5E

first to fly an operational mission—15 October—but by the end of November, both were on combat ops.

The first few encounters with the enemy came out well for the 55th Fighter Group, but this good fortune did not last long. On 9 November, two Lightnings were lost, on the 13th seven ships failed to return to the group's base at Nuthampstead, and on the 29th seven more planes were lost to bring the total losses for the month to eighteen. Another four Lightnings managed to struggle home only to be written off. The alarming factor was that many of the aircraft that did not return were a result of mechanical failure rather than enemy action.

Northern Europe is cursed with some of the worst flying weather in the world, especially during the winter months. Heavy cloud cover, cold weather and a pervasive dampness are a way of life. In addition, the bombers flew at altitudes up to 30,000 feet with the fighters often well above this. Outside temperatures of 60 degrees below zero were common.

Lieutenant Colonel Mark Hubbard, a one time commander of the 20th had this to say: "As an air to air fighter, I would have to rank the P-38 behind the P-51, P-47, Me 109 and FW 190. Below 20,000 feet it could hold its own but we didn't use it there." The old problem of compressibility also limited the maneouverability at high altitudes, and this put the pilots who flew the P-38 at a disadvantage."

On the way home from a bomber escort mission on 8 February, the 20th Fighter Group spotted a Bf 109 near a German airfield. One of the pilots made a pass but he wasn't able to fire because of a frosted windscreen, another common problem with the Lightning. Lieutenant James Morris then slid in behind the enemy fighter and opened fire. Pieces began to fly off the Bf 109 as Morris opened fire; the pilot bailed out of his stricken ship. Morris continued toward home, but near Sedan he sighted two more Luftwaffe fighters. The FW 190s had just taken off when the American zeroed in on one of the pair and fired two short bursts. The plane went down and Morris shifted his attention to the second FW 190. The chase took the planes through a low overcast and a rain cloud, but eventuallty he was able to get in a couple of bursts and the German spun in. Morris again pointed his aircraft toward England, but as he neared Denain, he saw a Bf 109 flying toward him. He hauled the P-38 around until he got on the tail of the German fighter and blasted his fourth victim of the day from the sky—a single mission record for the Eighth Air Force at the time.

The 3rd of March 1944 was a day the men of the Eighth had looked forward to for some time. The target for the bombers was to be the German capital itself. Unfortunately, the weather was bad enough that most of the planes were

[Top] Another 343rd ship, that of K.J. Sorace, awaits its next call to flight. This aircraft was names "Pitter Pat". [W. Smelzer]

[Center] Both the 20th and 55th [as well as the units to arrive later] used the geometric pattern. Eugene Geiger's ship [KI*V] belonged to the 55th Squadron. [E. Geiger]

[Left] The small size code letters dictated by the space available on the booms of the P-38 made some form of additional recognition necessary. In January 1944, large geometric shapes were added to the fin and rudder of Lightnings in the ETO. CL*T carries the circle. [W. Smelzer]

recalled. The 55th Fighter group had not received the recall and arrived over Berlin to meet the bombers. Lt. Col. Jack Jenkins was in the lead this day and he and his aircraft were the first American planes to fly above the city. When the bombers did not show up, Jenkins led the group home. On the way, one of his engines went out and he was forced to make the return journey at 12,000 feet on one mill. After the long, cold mission, Jenkins was so numb his crew chief had to help him from the cockpit.

On this same day, a third Lightning group went operational with the Eighth. The 364th had arrived in England in February, and had spent the intervening time getting ready for combat. During its first month on operations, it suffered the same high loss rate that had bedeviled the 20th and 55th - sixteen aircraft were lost.

Captain John Lowell was one member of the new group who did well from the start. On 6 March he led the group's 84th Squadron on an escort. After the Lightnings had turned for home, they ran into seven Bf 109s near Stienhuder Lake. Lowell led his flight on the attack and soon had blasted one of the German ships from the sky. He then turned his attention to a second victim, and after a few short bursts, saw this ship also go down with the canopy blown off and the landing gear starting to come down. On his next mission, two days later, Captain Lowell scored another double victory.

On 10 April, the 55th introduced a new look in the Lightning—a specially modified P-38, equipped with a plexiglass nose and room for a bombardier in this section, called the "droop-snoot". The aircraft was the result of experimentation and test by Colonels Cass Hough and Don Ostrander of Eighth Air Force to extend the capability of available equipment. The modification was made so that the P-38 could be used as a level bomber. The droop-snoot would act as lead ship and when it signaled, the entire formation following it would drop its load of bombs. The target for the 55th was the airfield at St. Dizier but when the planes approached the target area, it was obscured by a ground haze. Colonel Jenkins shifted the target to Coulommiers which was in the clear. After the bombs were dropped, Colonel Jenkins led one squadron down to strafe the field. On his first pass, the Colonel had his windscreen fogged up and he had to pull up for a go around. On this second pass the defenders were ready and opened up with every thing they had. Jenkins' and his wingman were hit and hit again. Jenkins bellied his ship in

[Top] Colonel Barton Russell's "Black Bart" bellied in in England. The commander of the 20th's ship displays the simulated Droop-snoot markings used by the P-38s from the spring of 1944. An eight inch white band was painted on the forward portion of the nose pod and the metal forward of this was polished. [D. Glover via D. Morris]

[Center] In the spring of 1944, the "Droop-snoot" first made its appearance. This ship, a converted P-38J had a complete bombardier's station built into the nose. This plane would act as the lead ship on level bombing missions. [80th Fighter Squadron Assoc.]

[Right] In March 1944 the 20th Fighter Group adopted group markings with the addition of yellow spinners and forward engine nacelles. These markings were also added to the Droop-snoot flown by the outfit. [R. Englehart]

The day before the D-Day Invasion, the Lightnings of the Eighth and Ninth received special markings. Because of its unique planform, it was the fighter used to patrol over the convoys heading for Normandy. The stripes were alternately white and black. Soon after D-Day, they were removed from the upper surfaces of most aircraft. [R. Englehart]

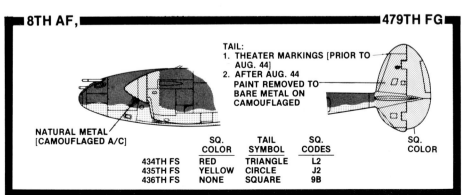

8TH AF, 479TH FG

TAIL:
1. THEATER MARKINGS [PRIOR TO AUG. 44]
2. AFTER AUG. 44
PAINT REMOVED TO BARE METAL ON CAMOUFLAGED

NATURAL METAL [CAMOUFLAGED A/C]

SQ. COLOR

	SQ. COLOR	TAIL SYMBOL	SQ. CODES
434TH FS	RED	TRIANGLE	L2
435TH FS	YELLOW	CIRCLE	J2
436TH FS	NONE	SQUARE	9B

and was taken prisoner. The 20th also flew its first droop-snoot mission later the same afternoon against Gutersloh, Germany. Both groups did relatively well on their assigned targets. The mission demonstrated the Lightning could be used effectively as a medium altitude bomber. Over the next several months, droop-snoot missions were flown regularly.

In April, the Eighth initiated **JACKPOT,** a systematic plan for attacks on German airfields. Under the plan, Germany was divided into sectors of several hundred square miles each. An individual fighter group was assigned one of these in northern and one in southern Germany. All that had to be done to give each group its target was announce either **JACKPOT A or B** (northern or southern Germany respectively).

The first full scale **JACKPOT** came on 15 April. The 364th was one of the groups assigned but at this stage in its career, it had little experience in ground strafing. Colonel Roy Osborn, group commander had this to say about the mission: "When we got to our assigned area, the whole group hit the deck and began shooting everything in sight. Flak was generally bad over the whole area; in addition flights became widely separated, navigation of some misfired, and they found themselves over the outskirts of large well defended cities such as Hamburg and Bremen. Airfields were crossed haphazardly, in most cases there were no aircraft as targets but only light flak positions throwing a withering fire at us. Eventually, with flights and elements scattered, the group withdrew, some came back through the clouds, some on the deck over the North Sea. Because of the weather only 36 aircraft reached the assigned area and got to the deck. Out of these, 23 were hit by light flak, seven of these were lost. We claimed four German planes but only two of these were on the ground."

When the problems developed with the Lightning, the call had gone out to Lockheed to find solutions. The company sent one of its top test pilots, Tony Levier, to England to investigate and report. He arrived in early 1944 and immediately began test flights to determine as much as he could about the problems and possible solutions to them. The problems were brought home quite vividly on his first test hop when his right engine blew and Levier had to set the ship down at a B-26 base.

The problem with controlling the high altitude dive of the P-38 had been found back in the States by this time, and Levier went to the Lockheed modification center near Belfast to pick up one of the Lightnings equipped with the special dive flap. He tested the ship there until he was satisfied he knew just what the plane would do. He brought the plane back to England and began a series of deomonstrations at the various bases where the P-38s were stationed.

At Kings Cliffe, home of the 20th, he took the plane up to 20,000 feet and then dived straight down at the Officer's Club. The pilots on the ground fully expected to see their club go up in a huge blast when the P-38 crashed, but Levier eased the plane out of the dive. After a series of single-engine maneuvers, he brought it in to a most appreciative audience. The single-engine portion of the program was especially important for it showed the Lightning could do almost as much on one engine as it could with two if it was handled properly. Slow rolls and inverted flight with a feathered prop convinced the pilots the Lightning was not the killer they believed it to be.

Early in May, 400 sets of the new dive flaps were loaded aboard a C-54 and dispatched from the States to the Lockheed facility in Ireland. Unfortunately, an RAF pilot intercepted the plane before it reached its destination. He

Another ship of the 392nd Squadron in France. This plane was flown by Captain H. Hartig. [R. Dillon via W. Hess]

Jimmy Paschell and his aircraft at a base on the continent in November 1944. He flew with the 392nd squadron, 367th Group. [R. Dillon via W. Hess]

Another war-time commander of the 20th Fighter Group was Colonel H. J. Rau shown here beside his "Gentle Annie". [U.S. Air Force]

mistook the transport for an FW 200 and shot it down. It was almost two months before the dive flaps arrived after this, and by this point in time, the decision had already been made to phase the P-38 out of the Eighth Air Force.

During May, the role of the fighters changed from strategic targets to tactical ones. The long awaited invasion of Europe was near and missions flown by the Eighth were aimed at paving the way. Using the same grip structure as **JACKPOT**, a determined attack on German transportation was instituted by the fighters. This plan, under the name **CHATTANOOGA**, resulted in the destruction of 91 locomotives on the first day it was implemented (21 May). The 55th Fighter Group accounted for fifteen of these and also was credited with six German planes on the ground and another in the air. The group paid heavily for this success for six ships failed to return.

The last P-38 unit to join the Eighth Air Force was the 479th. It arrived in England in mid-May and by the 26th of the month, was declared operational. Also during May, two Lightning groups became operational with the Ninth Air Force in England. This brought the strength of the Ninth to three P-38 groups. The 474th had begun combat operations in late April followed by the 367th and 370th on 9 May.

Though the Lightning groups of both the Eighth and Ninth flew a number of missions during the invasion, it was a time of little action. The P-38s, partly because of their unique planform, were assigned the task of protecting the fleets headed for Normandy. Each of the seven groups flew nine missions on D-Day (in squadron strength) and this type of activity continued for several days after the landings. The pilots were glad when the deadly dullness of fleet patrol ended and they could get back into the action.

The dive flap kits had begun to reach the combat units by late June. One

The 479th Fighter Group flew the Lightning longer than any other Eighth Air Force Fighter Group. Here, Captain Moser poses before his camouflaged "Tiger Lilly" [479th Fighter Group]

Major Duffie and his "Give 'M Hell for H.L." of the 479th Fighter Group. This unit continued to fly the Lightning until the end of September 1944. [479th Fighter Group]

Colonel Jack Jenkins, commander of the 55th Fighter Group in front of his "Texas Ranger". [W. Smelzer]

evening in early July, Art Heiden was flying the number three position to Colonel Cy Wilson, commander of the 20th. Wilson's ship was equipped with dive flaps and Heiden recalled what happened on the mission: "Just after sundown we arrived on station near Paris and were confronted with a large gaggle of Me 109s. Without hesitation Colonel Wilson cut out a single 109 which took the usual evasive action and headed straight down. To this German's surprise and horror, the Colonel rolled into a dive after him and tail-gated him almost vertically into the darkness below. My aircraft was not modified so it was all I could do to try and follow the action without getting into compressibility problems. I lost sight of the two planes but eventually there was a sudden splash of light as an aircraft hit the ground. I called Wilson to be sure he was all right and received the welcomer reply that he was fine and had us in sight. Later he remarked that going down after the Me 109 was just like taking candy from a baby."

The 20th and 55th flew their last P-38 missions on 21 July. Eight days later, the 364th joined the other two groups in the Mustang. Only the 479th continued in the big Lockheed fighter in the Eighth.

In the Ninth Air Force, the Lightning was used effectively as a ground attack machine. The concentrated firepower in the nose suited the aircraft well for this role. Even so, a big fight would develop on occasion between the P-38 pilots and those of the Luftwaffe. The 367th Fighter Group had just finished a dive bombing mission when it received a call for assistance from another unit then under attack. Among the men who responded to this call was Captain Lawrence Blumer. Soon after joining the battle, he got on the tail of an FW 190 that was trying to down another P-38. Blumer gave the enemy ship a good burst and the plane broke into flames. He caught a second FW flying alone and sent it down in flames. He then climbed and dove on his third victim of the day. The German plane disintegrated in an explosion that Blumer's wingman thought had caught the American ship. The P-38 soon emerged from the

Lightnings of the 367th Fighter Group on the flight line a Jouvencourt. The ship in the foreground is "Arkansas Traveler". [R. Dillon via W. Hess]

By the spring of 1944, the aircraft of the Eighth Air Force started to operate in natural metal finish. Markings that had appeared in white on camouflaged ships were now painted in black. [Air Force Museum]

smoke and debris with no damage. By this time the Luftwaffe pilots were trying to get away as best they could. In the melee, the Captain shot down his fourth and fifth aircraft of the day. Blumer thus joined the ranks of men who had made ace in a day. All together the pilots of the 367th claimed twenty air victories on the mission.

The 479th began conversion to the Mustang in early September but the process was rather slow. By the 26th of the month there were still a number of P-38s on strength and missions were often flown with both types of aircraft. The mission of 26 September was such a mixed mission to the Munster/Haltern area. The group was soon vectored to a large German formation and a big battle broke out. The 479th downed 29 German aircraft in the action. This was a fitting end to the combat career of the Lightning with the Eighth Air Force for two days, later, the group completed its change to P-51s.

The Ninth continued to operate the Lightning as a fighter bomber for some time. In February 1945 the 367th and 370th converted to Thunderbolts and Mustangs respectively. Only the 474th continued to fly the P-38 until the end of the war.

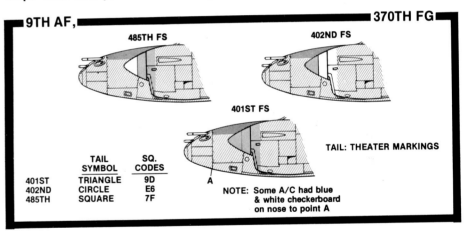

9TH AF, **370TH FG**

485TH FS   402ND FS

401ST FS

TAIL: THEATER MARKINGS

	TAIL SYMBOL	SQ. CODES
401ST	TRIANGLE	9D
402ND	CIRCLE	E6
485TH	SQUARE	7F

NOTE: Some A/C had blue & white checkerboard on nose to point A

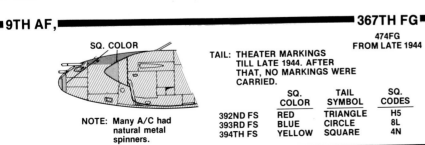

9TH AF, **367TH FG**

474FG FROM LATE 1944

SQ. COLOR

TAIL: THEATER MARKINGS TILL LATE 1944. AFTER THAT, NO MARKINGS WERE CARRIED.

	SQ. COLOR	TAIL SYMBOL	SQ. CODES
392ND FS	RED	TRIANGLE	H5
393RD FS	BLUE	CIRCLE	8L
394TH FS	YELLOW	SQUARE	4N

NOTE: Many A/C had natural metal spinners.

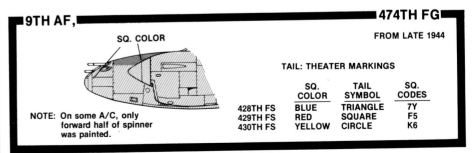

9TH AF, **474TH FG**

FROM LATE 1944

SQ. COLOR

TAIL: THEATER MARKINGS

	SQ. COLOR	TAIL SYMBOL	SQ. CODES
428TH FS	BLUE	TRIANGLE	7Y
429TH FS	RED	SQUARE	F5
430TH FS	YELLOW	CIRCLE	K6

NOTE: On some A/C, only forward half of spinner was painted.

Behind the remains of a German aircraft, a P-38 of the 370th Fighter Group sits on a base in Belgium in December 1944. [W. Hess]

Though white was the assigned color applied to the spinners and forward cowls of the P-38s of the 364th Fighter Group, there was still room for variation. N2*K was flown by a pilot who must have been a ladies man for there was a different name on both sides of the nose and on both cowls. [D. Robinson]

Pacific Lightnings

For the United States, war in the Pacific came with the suddeness of a bolt of Lightning out of a partially cloudy sky. The Japanese attack on Pearl Harbor was directed at the destruction of American sea and air power, and most objectives in this line were met. Only the American carriers escaped destruction—a fact that would haunt the attackers in the future. The next six months were a time of holding, then retreat, and then defeat for the Allies as Japan expanded its domination of virtually the entire South Pacific. The logical extension of these conquests was the continent of Australia, and by the spring of 1942 only the capture of New Guinea, the closest large land mass to the northern coast of Australia, lay before the Japanese.

On 22 July, Japanese troops landed on the north Coast of New Guinea, at Gona and Buna Mission, to open the campaign against Port Moresby by land. The two villages were especially important for they marked the northern end of the Kokoda Trail—the one good passage across the Owen Stanleys. The Australian troops defending the area put up a stiff fight, but they were gradually forced back. By the middle of the following month, the forces of the Emperor had captured the airstrip at Kokoda on the crest of the mountains and stood poised for the final descent into Port Moresby.

At this crucial point, a new commander for the Allied Air Forces in Australia and New Guinea arrived on the scene—Major General George C. Kenney. One of his first official acts in his new job was to request fifty of the big Lockheed fighters and pilots to fly them.

When Kenney took command on 2 August, he had three American fighter groups (8th, 35th and 49th) with a total of 245 fighters. This was a paper strength for on checking, he found only 75 of the ships actually ready for combat. The remainder were awaiting salvage or repair. The planes he did have were P-39s and P-40s—aircraft that had fared poorly in combat against the Japanese. By replacing tired, worn commanders with fresher, more aggressive ones and by inbuing the pilots with a belief in themselves, he was able to help stop the advancing Japanese when they were within sight of their objective.

In late August, the first 25 P-38s and pilots arrived in Brisbane. The 39th Fighter Squadron (35th Fighter Group) was the first to get the new fighters when sixteen ships were flown up to Port Moresby. A major problem developed before the planes could be committed to combat. Leaks in the intercoolers in

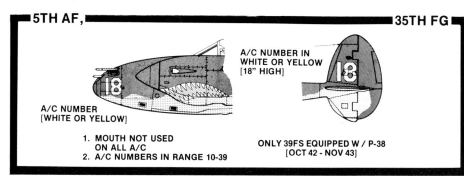

5TH AF, ━━━━━━━━━━━━━━━━━━━ 35TH FG

A/C NUMBER IN WHITE OR YELLOW [18" HIGH]

A/C NUMBER [WHITE OR YELLOW]

1. MOUTH NOT USED ON ALL A/C
2. A/C NUMBERS IN RANGE 10-39

ONLY 39FS EQUIPPED W / P-38 [OCT 42 - NOV 43]

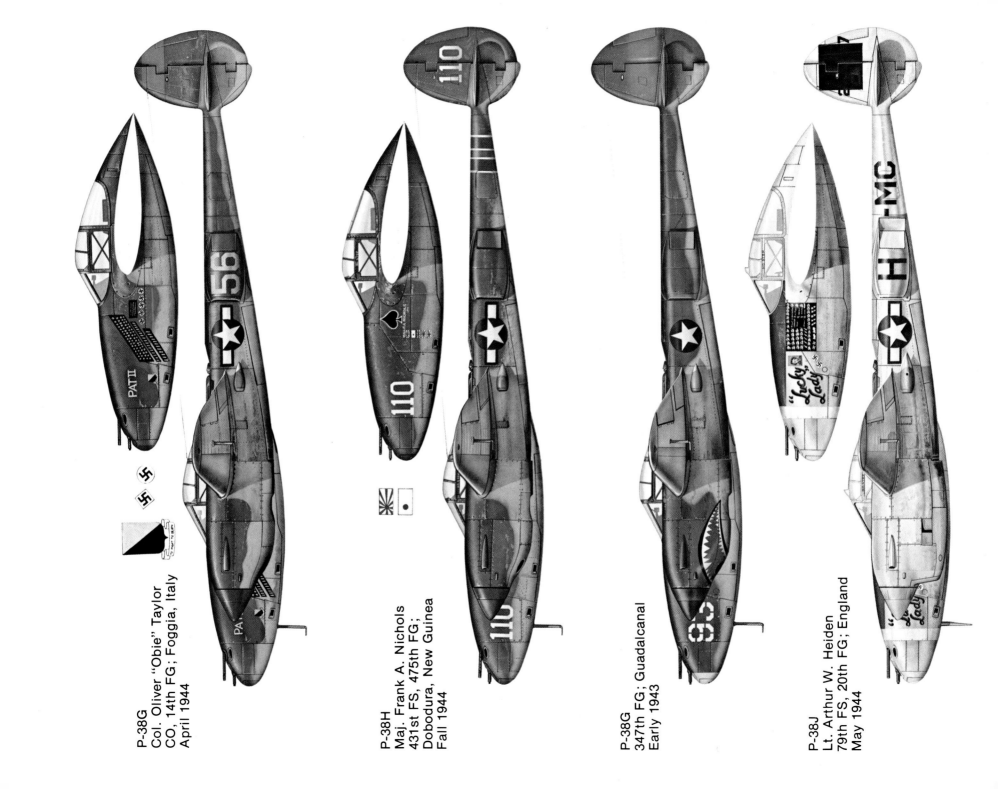

P-38G
Col. Oliver "Obie" Taylor
CO, 14th FG; Foggia, Italy
April 1944

P-38H
Maj. Frank A. Nichols
431st FS, 475th FG;
Dobodura, New Guinea
Fall 1944

P-38G
347th FG; Guadalcanal
Early 1943

P-38J
Lt. Arthur W. Heiden
79th FS, 20th FG; England
May 1944

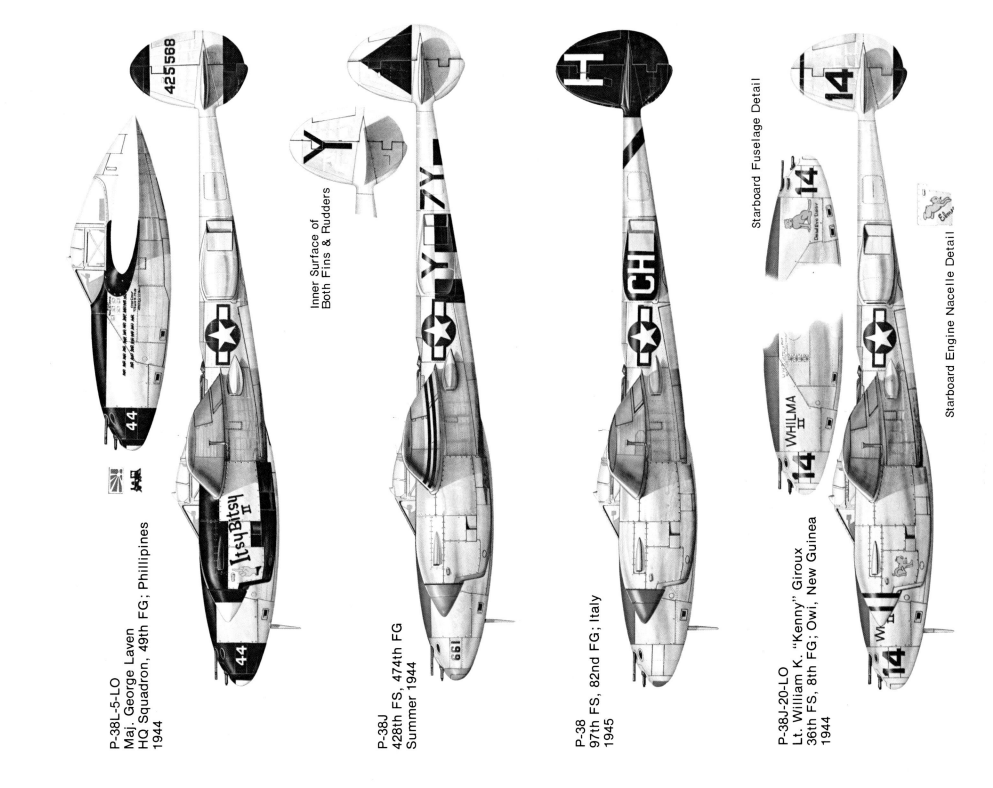

425568

44

Itsy Bitsy II

44

P-38L-5-LO
Maj. George Laven
HQ Squadron, 49th FG; Phillipines
1944

Inner Surface of
Both Fins & Rudders

Y

7Y

199

P-38J
428th FS, 474th FG
Summer 1944

H

CH

P-38
97th FS, 82nd FG; Italy
1945

Starboard Fuselage Detail

14

Dead Eye Daisy

WHILMA II

14

Elmer

14

WH

14

Starboard Engine Nacelle Detail

P-38J-20-LO
Lt. William K. "Kenny" Giroux
36th FS, 8th FG; Owi, New Guinea
1944

the leading edge of the wings were found, and this neccessitated an almost total rebuild of the wing. As a result, the P-38s weren't ready to go to war until the latter part of November. The Japanese had been driven back from Port Moresby by this time and Kenney's Fifth Air Force was established on the north Coast of New Guinea.

The pilots of the 39th were anxious for action. They flew frequent patrols over the big enemy air base at Lae, but no enemy fighters rose to meet them. Strangely enough, the radio frequency used by both sides was the same. The Lightning pilots tried to taunt the Japanese pilots into coming up but even this didn't seem to work.

The 39th finally got the big fight it was looking for on 27 December when twelve P-38s were ordered to intercept a Japanese force headed toward Dobodura, the major base established on the north side of New Guinea. The American fighters, led by Captain Thomas J. Lynch, arrived over Dobo shortly after noon and soon spotted the inbound enemy bombers and fighter escort. All together there were some 25 ships in the formation. The American fighters broke down into three flights and went on the attack. When the battle was over, fifteen Japanese ships were downed with no loss to the Americans. Three of the American pilots claimed two victories including Lynch, Kenneth Sparks and Richard Bong. Though the tactics used by the Americans were less than perfect, the success of the 39th sent morale sky high and demonstrated how well the big new fighter could do in combat.

In early January, enough Lightnings were available to equip a second fighter squadron. The 9th Fighter Squadron (49th Fighter Group) was the selected unit and several of the pilots assigned to the 39th transferred to the new squadron, including Dick Bong. The old hands of the 9th had been equipped with the P-40, and, though it was supposedly inferior to the Japanese planes, were reluctant to change their nimble mounts for the much larger Lightning. The success of the 39th and a test hop in the twin-boomed fighter convinced them that here was one hell of an airplane.

In February 1943, the 8th Fighter Group was forced to withdraw from New Guinea to Australia. The outfit had entered combat during the campaign around Milne Bay, on the eastern tip of the island, in September. In December and January, malaria hit the pilots and ground crew members in epidemic proportions. There were simply not enough men to continue operations. While in Australia, one of the squadrons assigned to the 8th, the 80th Fighter Squadron, traded in its P-39s for the P-38. The healing and conversion process lasted almost two months, but by the end of March, the squadron returned to action. The new Lightning outfit scored its first victories on the 11th of April

[Top] The first unit to receive the P-38 in the SWPA was the 39th Fighter Squadron. The big ship was desperately needed in the drive to rid the skies over New Guinea of the Japanese. [80th Fighter Squadron Association]

[Center] The 39th had a number of men who became aces while flying the Ligntning. One of them was Richard Smith. All seven of his kills came while mounted in the P-38. [R. Smith]

[Right] Unlike the European Theater where the national insignia was usually seen with a yellow surround until the introduction of the star and bar configuration, aircraft in the SWPA carried only the roundel. [S. Woods]

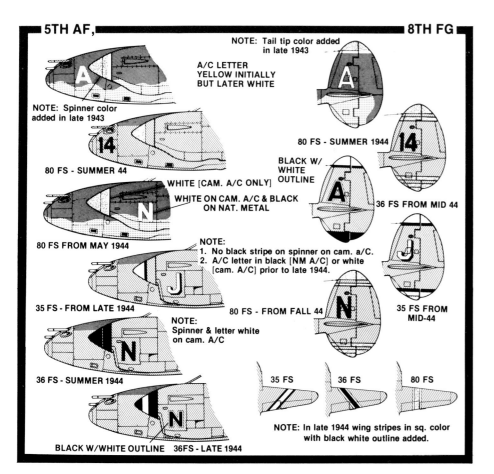

NOTE: Tail tip color added in late 1943

A/C LETTER YELLOW INITIALLY BUT LATER WHITE

NOTE: Spinner color added in late 1943

80 FS - SUMMER 44

80 FS - SUMMER 1944

80 FS - SUMMER 1944

BLACK W/ WHITE OUTLINE

WHITE [CAM. A/C ONLY]

WHITE ON CAM. A/C & BLACK ON NAT. METAL

80 FS FROM MAY 1944

36 FS FROM MID 44

NOTE:
1. No black stripe on spinner on cam. a/c.
2. A/C letter in black [NM A/C] or white [cam. A/C] prior to late 1944.

35 FS - FROM LATE 1944

80 FS - FROM FALL 44

35 FS FROM MID-44

NOTE: Spinner & letter white on cam. A/C

36 FS - SUMMER 1944

35 FS   36 FS   80 FS

NOTE: In late 1944 wing stripes in sq. color with black white outline added.

BLACK W/WHITE OUTLINE   36FS - LATE 1944

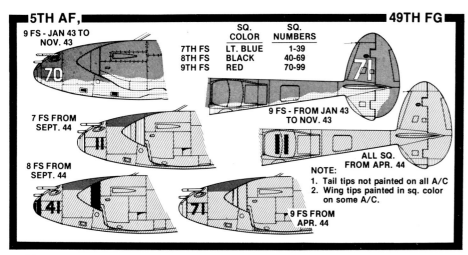

9 FS - JAN 43 TO NOV. 43

	SQ. COLOR	SQ. NUMBERS
7TH FS	LT. BLUE	1-39
8TH FS	BLACK	40-69
9TH FS	RED	70-99

7 FS FROM SEPT. 44

9 FS - FROM JAN 43 TO NOV. 43

8 FS FROM SEPT. 44

ALL SQ. FROM APR. 44

NOTE:
1. Tail tips not painted on all A/C
2. Wing tips painted in sq. color on some A/C.

9 FS FROM APR. 44

when Danny Roberts destroyed two and singles were registered by Leonides Mathers and Glenn Hope.

The battle of the Bismark Sea was fought in early March 1943. The Japanese tried to slip a major resupply convoy into Lae but the aircraft of the Fifth Air Force and the RAAF hit the ships over a two day period and when they were finished, the only thing left in the sea were well fed sharks. In addition to the sunk ships, the pilots of the Fifth entered claims for the destruction of 60 enemy planes. The P-38s of the 39th and the 9th Fighter Squadrons scored well during the period. General Order 53 of the Fifth Air Force showed the 39th with 77 victories and the 9th with 56 by the 20th of March. A number of these were the result of combat before the arrival of the Lightning, but many more were scored after the big Lockheed fighter made its appearance.

On the day after the Battle of the Bismark Sea, General Kenney headed for Washington and a round of conferences on the progress of the air war in the SWPA. High on his list of items for discussion was a demand for more P-38s. Some 31 years after this, General Kenney wrote; "When I was in Washington, General Arnold said he could give me enough P-38s for a new group but no personnel, air or ground. I told him to give me the planes and I would take care of the men.

"About the middle of May (after he returned to the SWPA) General Arnold sent word that the new ships were on the way. Between then and the time I got the planes, I had to find the men to staff the new group. I had closed a lot of weather stations and caretaker units at fields all over Australia that had been built in case the Japanese invaded the country. I also enlisted a lot of Chinese cooks and stewards in Australia who had been rescued from sunken ships and thereby released more men for my new fighter group. I robbed the rear areas of all qualified pilots and put Major George Prentiss, the original CO of the 39th Squadron, in charge of getting the 475th ready for war. Intensive flying and gunnery training and familiarization flights over the part of New Guinea we controlled went on until August. At that time the 475th Fighter Group was pronounced ready for combat."

On 21 June, thirteen ships from the 80th Fighter Squadron flew an escort mission for B-25s scheduled to drop supplies at Guadagasel. Shortly after the Mitchells drop their loads, the call came in that Japanese aircraft were in the vicinity and the Lightnings made a wide circle to intercept. The individual

In January 1943, the 9th Fighter Squadron became the second unit in the Fifth Air Force to equip with the P-38. [S. Woods]

[Right] When the 9th converted to the P-38, Sidney Woods was flying with the outfit. Later he served with the Eight Air Force and ended the war with ten victories. [S. Woods]

[Right Below] The Japanese also introduced a new fighter, the KI-61, in New Guinea. Though a good plane, its armament was not match for the Lightning when combat took place from this angle. [R. Smith]

four-ship flights were somewhat separated and when contact was made, it came at several points. The enemy force numbered some thirty planes including some bombers, but the action revolved in fighter to fighter combat, and resulted in claims of thirteen. Corky Smith took top honors for the day with three Zeros. Three other pilots scored doubles, including a pair by George Welch. Welch had been at Pearl Harbor the day the Japanese attacked and was one of the few American pilots to make it into the air. In the action he knocked four of the attackers from the sky to register the first American victories of the war.

The latter part of July was a period of big scoring days for all the squadrons. On the 21st, the 39th and 80th were escorting B-25s on a raid to Bogadjim when a force of 25-30 Japanese fighters came on the scene. Each of the two American P-38 squadrons scored eleven victories with top honors going to Jay Robbins of the 80th who ran up three Zeros. Robbins ended the war as the top ace in the 80th with a total of 22 victories. Three pilots from the 80th and two from the 39th scored doubles and ten other pilots knocked one plane each from the air. Two days later, the same two squadrons were in another battle in the same area and added a total of twelve more Japanese aircraft to their scoreboards.

The 9th, and Dick Bong, ran into a Japanese formation on 26 July. Ten Lightnings joined combat over the Markham Valley, northwest of Lae with some twenty Oscars and Tonys. In the action that followed, Bond flamed two of the enemy fighters and saw two others disintigrate in mid-air when his bullets struck. He added another Oscar two days later to bring his victory total to sixteen.

A new advance base also came into play by the end of July. Near the Japanese bases at Salamaua and Lae, the American engineers had built a new strip from which to launch raids in support of the planned conquest of the area. The name of the base was Tsili-Tsili but Kenney much preferred to call it Marilinan. As he had said: "In case the Nips should take us out, somebody might throw that Tsili-Tsili thing back at me." Elements of the 35th Fighter Group moved in on 21 July and the first fighters landed on the evening of the 26th.

Though enemy air strength had been negated at Lae and Salamaua, the Japanese still had a major base at Wewak. This had to be neutralized before any operations could begin against Lae and Salamaua and recon planes kept close watch on activity there. In mid-August, a major build-up was spotted at Wewak and plans were made for a series of raids. By this time the 475th was ready for combat and participated in these raids with great success. Between its first operational mission on 16 August and the end of the month the 475th claimed 53 enemy planes, most over the Wewak area. The other Lightning units also scored well during this period. The 80th scored 22 victories and the total claims by the bombers and fighters of the Fifth came 309 aircraft on the

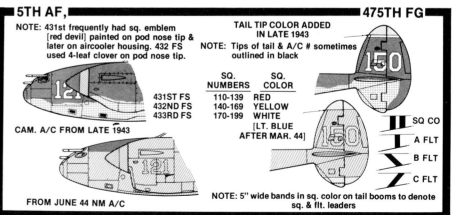

5TH AF, **475TH FG**

NOTE: 431st frequently had sq. emblem [red devil] painted on pod nose tip & later on aircooler housing. 432 FS used 4-leaf clover on pod nose tip.

CAM. A/C FROM LATE 1943

FROM JUNE 44 NM A/C

431ST FS
432ND FS
433RD FS

TAIL TIP COLOR ADDED IN LATE 1943

NOTE: Tips of tail & A/C # sometimes outlined in black

SQ. NUMBERS	SQ. COLOR
110-139	RED
140-169	YELLOW
170-199	WHITE [LT. BLUE AFTER MAR. 44]

SQ CO
A FLT
B FLT
C FLT

NOTE: 5" wide bands in sq. color on tail booms to denote sq. & flt. leaders

[Left] Both Fighter Squadron aircraft on the flight line. [80th Fighter Squadron Assoc.]

[Center] A P-38 of the 475th nosed over on the strip at Biak Island. [Air Force Museum]

[Bottom] 475th dispersal area at Dobodura. Though the group normally used aircraft numbers in the 100-200 range, this was not always the case as seen by number 73. [H. Brown]

ground or in the air. The back of the Japanese air power in the area was broken and both Lae and Salamaua fell the following month.

Though General Kenney would have equipped every group with the P-38 if he could, the demands of the other theaters limited the number of Lightnings he could get his hands on. P-47s were, however arriving in the SWPA and a decision was made to concentrate the P-38s in the 475th Fighter Group and the 80th Fighter Squadron (8th Group). The 39th and the 9th Squadrons were to convert to the Thunderbolt. The men who had been flying the Lightning were less than enchanted with the prospect of the shift in mounts. Both completed the conversion in November 1943. Ralph Wandrey of the 9th recalled: "Whenever a '38 came in to land, we ordered the new boys (Thunderbolt jockeys fresh from the States) to stand at attention and remove their caps—just to teach them the proper respect for a real airplane!"

With the fall of Lae and Salamaua and the effective neutralization of Wewak, the attention of the fighters of the Fifth turned to the major Japanese base at Rabaul, on New Britain. From September until the end of the year many of the air battles took place over this area. The long distances involved meant the Lightning bore the brunt of the action. Here, the two engines of the P-38 made the pilots especially happy. Many men made it home on a single engine after combat or a mechanical problem developed—men who would have been lost if they had been in a single-engine plane.

Allied troops invaded New Britain on 26 December and the P-38s of the 475th and the 80th provided much of the air support. On the 27th, Captain Thomas McGuire, eventually the second leading U.S. fighter ace, led the 431st Squadron on a patrol over Cape Gloucester when an inbound force of 25-30 Vals was spotted. In his combat report, he stated: "My flight caught up with them as they were in their diving run and forced them to drop their bombs at from 8,000/10,000 feet and they did no damage, with the exception of one which closed right in on a destroyer and made a hit. The destroyer sank as a result of this attack. I got a short burst at one Val and it started smoking, then went straight down and crashed. I chased the Vals as they went right down to the water and then headed along the shore. I made about eight passes at different aircraft with no success, but finally got right on the tail of one and, giving him several bursts, he exploded. After a couple of passes at other aircraft, I got a stern shot at another Val. This one crashed into the water. At this time my second element had lost me completely and, after I had made a pass at a Val which started smoking and was headed inland, I was joined by a P-47 from the 36th Squadron (8th Fighter Group). Together we attacked this aircraft again and I got directly behind him, at minimum altitude, and gave him a good burst. Pieces flew off and I saw the Val blow up just as he hit a tree."

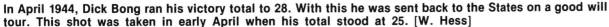

In April 1944, Dick Bong ran his victory total to 28. With this he was sent back to the States on a good will tour. This shot was taken in early April when his total stood at 25. [W. Hess]

John Loisel, a later commander of the 475th, flew "Screaming Kid". At this time, the plane carried eight of his eventual eleven victories. [J. Loisel]

Though McGuire entered claims for fours Vals, the last one was awarded to the Jug pilot. The 475th had a total of 46 victories during December, most in the closing days of the month.

The 80th Squadron entered claims for eighteen aircraft in December-again, the bulk of these came toward the end of the month. This was also a time of sadness for the squadron for its leader, Major Edward Cragg was lost in combat. Shortly after Cragg shot down a Tojo, his fifteenth victory, he was seen being chased by a Japanese fighter. Lt. Adams made a pass at the enemy fighter and shot him down, but Major Cragg entered a cloud and never reappeared.

The first half of 1944 saw the Allied forces move up the northern coast of New Guinea as they drove the Japanese back. Hollandia, Wadke Biak and Owi became the home of the P-38s as the war leapfrogged its way westward. Scores continued to rise as the Japanese rose to meet the American fighters on occasion but by the start of summer, there was little enemy activity left in New Guinea. More Lightnings became available to the Fifth Air Force and by May the 9th had reconverted to the ship. Also, the entire 8th Fighter Group (35th, 36th Squadrons) was mounted in P-38s by this time. This brought the strength of the Fifth to seven squadrons.

Further to the east, the Thirteenth Air Force also operated Lightnings. The Air Force had been formed in January 1943 from units that had arrived earlier for the protection of New Caledonia and, later, the protection of Guadalcanal. In January 1943 only the 339th Fighter Squadron was equipped with P-38s and never more than a few of these were available at any one time. The ship did, however, offer the Thirteenth the long range and high altitude capability it needed.

The 339th Fighter Squadron participated in one of the most incredible missions of the war on 18 April 1943. The reason began several thousand miles away where U.S. Navy personnel at Dutch Harbor intercepted a coded Japanese message that stated Admiral Isoroku Yamamoto, the planner of the attack on Pearl Harbor, was to make an inspection trip to Bougainville and other bases in the area. A portion of this trip was to be by air and the Americans planned a daring intercept during this time. The Lightning was the only plane available capable of flying the long range involved, so the task of carrying out the mission fell on Major John W. Mitchell, CO of the 339th.

Every tiny detail of the mission was worked out in advance so that when eighteen Lightnings took off from Henderson Field on the 18th, the chances were relatively good—provided all the calculations were accurate. It was a tremenduous job to plot the course of the Japanese planes and then determine the exact time when the Americans would intercept after flying an indirect course over open ocean of 435 miles. Just as the American fighters arrived on station the Japanese formation appeared right on schedule.

Yamamoto and his second in command were flying in separate Betty bombers. Mitchell's plan called for a flight of four ships to attack the bombers while the other planes provided cover and took on the escort. Thomas Lanphier, Jr., Rex T. Barber, Besby T. Holmes, and Raymond K. Hines made up the attack flight. The post-mission report describes the action: "When Lanphier and Barber were within one mile of contact, their attack was observ

[Left] Many of the pilots who were assigned to the 475th came from the three squadrons then flying the P-38 in New Guinea. One of the men who came from the 9th Squadron was John Hood. He finished the war with five victories. [H. Brown]

[Below Left] When General Kenny got the go-ahead to form a new P-38 outfit, the 475th, the man he selected to head it was George Prentice. [J. Loisel]

ed by the enemy. The bombers nosed down, one starting a 360 degree turn dive, the other going out and away toward the shoreline; the Zeros dropped their belly tanks and three peeled down, in a string to intercept Lanphier. When he saw that he could not reach the bomber he turned up and into the Zeros, exploding the first, and firing into the others as they passed. By this time he had reached 6,000 feet, so he nosed over, and went down to the tree tops after his escaping objective. He came into it broadside — firing his burst—a wing flew off and the plane went flaming to earth."

"Barber had gone in with Lanphier on the initial attack. He went for one of the bombers but its maneuvers caused him to overshoot a little. He whipped back, however, and although pursued by Zeros, caught the bomber and destroyed it. When he fired, the tail section flew off, the bomber turned over on its back and plummetted to earth.

"By this time, Holmes had been able to drop his tank and with Hine, came in to ward off the Zeros who were pursueing Barber. The flight was on its way out of the combat area (in the neighborhood of enemy bases at Kahili, Ballale and Shortland-Faisi) when Holmes noticed a stray bomber near Moila Point flying low over the water. He dove on it, his bursts getting it smoking in the left engine; Hine also shot at it and Barber polished it off with a burst in the fuselage. The bomber exploded right in my face! A piece of the plane flew off, cut through his left wing and knocked out his left inter-cooler and other chunks left streaks on his wing—so close was his attack driven home." The 339th received credit for three Bettys and three Zeros on the mission for the loss of one pilot (Hine).

During the spring and early summer, the Japanese still flew bombing attacks against the Americans. On 16 June, a large force of Vals escorted by Zeros was intercepted by a mixed force of P-38s, P-39s and P-40s. Eleven of the ships were knocked from the sky by the Americans including six by Lt. Murray J. Shubin of the 339th Fighter Squadron. This feat was the only time in the Pacific when a P-38 pilot scored five or more victories on a single mission.

Though the Thirteenth Air Force still had an average of less than twenty Lightnings on hand during the summer of 1943, this total rose to fifty by the end of the year. Also during the summer, the mission of the Air Force changed from defense to offense as the Allied forces moved up the Solomons, Russells, and Bougainville. The ships supported these landings and then helped support the efforts of the Fifth Air Force in the neutralization of Rabaul. In 1944, the aircraft of the Thirteenth shifted their bases of operation to New Guinea to help clear the last Japanese from the island.

Above the Mediterranean Part II

Flight line for the 433rd Squadron at Dobodura. At the time of this shot, the squadron had adopted the practice of painting the squadron color [white] on the rear half of the spinner. [via R. Anderson]

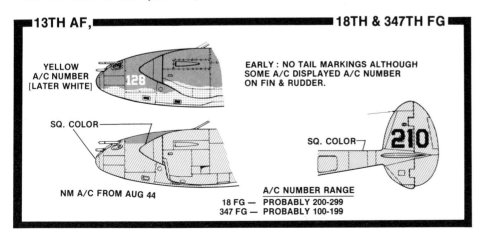

■13TH AF,■   ■18TH & 347TH FG■

YELLOW
A/C NUMBER
[LATER WHITE]

SQ. COLOR

NM A/C FROM AUG 44

EARLY : NO TAIL MARKINGS ALTHOUGH
SOME A/C DISPLAYED A/C NUMBER
ON FIN & RUDDER.

SQ. COLOR

A/C NUMBER RANGE
18 FG — PROBABLY 200-299
347 FG — PROBABLY 100-199

The activation of the Fifteenth Air Force on 1 November 1943 was a move on the part of Ameriican Strategic Air Force planners to strengthen the prosecution of the air war against German's war industry. The new organization would be able to hit targets in southern Germany, the Balkans, and Central Europe—targets out of the range of bombers flying from England. Also, it was hoped to spread the defenses of Germany and enable raids to be carried out almost every day. Among the units assigned to the new Air Force were the three P-38 units already in the theater—the 1st, 14th and 82nd. By January 1944, all three Lightning fighter groups had moved to new bases in the area around Foggia, Italy. This put the groups closer to the action and meant shorter flights to escort the bombers.

The 48th Fighter Squadron (14th Fighter Group) had a big day on 2 April. Twelve Lightnings, led by Lt. McGuyrt, were escorting bombers to Steyr, Austria when enemy aircraft intercepted. A flight of Re 2001s attacked the bombers and were engaged by the Lightnings. Soon, other enemy planes including Bf 110s, Me 210s, Bf 109s and FW 190s joined the battle and a large dog-fight ensued. The Americans didn't lose any ships in the battle, but the German and Italian formation did not fare as well. Twelve confirmed victories were scored including a triple by Lt. Lindstrom and a double by McGuyrt.

Five days later, the 14th was again involved in a big air battle while on an escort mission to Mestre, Italy. Lt. Lou Benne was leading a flight on the mission, and, after the bombers had cleared the target area, took his flight back into the area to engage the enemy fighters in the area. He led his ships on a diving attack on some Bf 109s below him, but was forced to break off when enemy fighters made a head-on pass. In this action, Benne became separated from the other three Lightnings. As he climbed to rejoin them, he spotted two Bf 109s about to make an attack on another flight of P-38s. He dropped the nose of his fighter and pulled up dead astern of one of the German ships. He opened fire and saw the left wing of the Messerschmitt begin to buckle. Benne continued to fire along the entire length of the fuselage and the enemy plane disintegrated.

As he looked around for the second Bf 109, Benne expected to see it diving out of range. Instead, the German ship was still maneuvering for position to attack the formation of Lightnings. Slipping over behind this Bf 109, Benne pulled the nose of his ship up slightly and fired at the plane until it rolled over and went down in flames. All together, the squadron downed six German ships on the mission.

For almost a year, the Americans had been trying to knock out the oil refineries at Ploesti. Mission after mission was targeted for the B-24s and B-17s to hit this vital target. Still the facility was in production in June 1944. At this point some one up the line had the idea to send in two groups of Lightnings to knock the refinery out by dive-bombing. The group selected for the actual dive-bombing was the 82nd and the 1st was slated to cover these

planes. Thirty nine ships from the 82nd and another 39 from the 1st took part. Though the target was hit with some damage and 29 enemy planes were destroyed in the air (24 by the 1st Fighter Group) the price was extremely high. The 82nd had eight ships fail to return to base while the 1st reported fourteen ships either lost or missing. Almost 30 percent of the P-38s who went on the mission were lost.

On 22 July, the 82nd went on a shuttle mission to Russia along with aircraft from the 14th. On the way there, the formation came across an airfield with a large number of planes parked on it. In the strafing attack that followed, forty planes were destroyed. On the way home on the 26th of the month, a big fight broke out with enemy fighters and twelve of them were shot down.

On the second and final shuttle mission to Russia a short time later, Capt. Richard Willsie had his left engine shot out by groundfire. He called his flight to let them know he was going in. Suddenly, the voice of Richard Andrews crackled in his ears. "Pick a good spot. I'm coming down after you." True to his word, the young pilot from Portland, Oregon set his P-38 down into the mushy furrows of a Rumanian pasture as near to Willsie's plane as he could. Willsie set his own plane on fire and then sprinted to the waiting Andrews. Both pilots discarded their chutes and crammed themselves into the one cockpit. Two and a half hours later they landed safely in Russia after a long stretch of blind flying through heavy rain.

With passing of summer, enemy opposition began to drop off. The three Lightning units still flew escort, but there were many missions where no enemy planes were even spotted much less joined in combat. Typically, after September 1944, the 82nd scored only four more victories for the remainder of the war.

Between 18 August and early November, the Fifteenth Air Force flew more than 35 tactical missions in Yugoslavia and Hungary in support of the Russian advance. The requests came through Balkan Air Force were based on the needs for air effort to trap and destroy the enemy forces in the area. The results were good and resulted in the destruction of some 621 enemy planes, quite a bit of railroad rolling stock, motor vehicles and German soldiers during the period. The mission of 7 November was, however, quite a different story all together. The mission was flown by the 82nd Fighter Group under the leadership of Colonel C.T. Edwinson, but there is nothing on the official group records about it. The only record located was a highly classified (since declassified) series of messages at high levels. The "Official Position" of the events is contained in one of these: "Early this month, a squadron of 15th AAF

[Top] For long range missions, the P-38 carried fuel in the large tanks carried beneath the wings. [L. Carr]

[Center] Over shorter distances, the ship could carry a healthy load of 500 pound bombs. [L. Carr]

Droop-snoots were also employed in the Med. "Hellza Droppin" belonged to the 82nd Fighter Group. It carries the codes of the 95th Squadron. [L. Carr]

[Left] Ships of the 1st Fighter Group come back from a mission and prepare to land in Italy. [W. Hess]

Toward the end of the war, aerial combat was a rare thing for the Lightnings so other targets were hit. In this shot, Lt. Can of the 82nd Fighter Group destroys one of the 30 Locomotives claimed by Fifteenth Air Force Fighters on 1 March 1945. [L. Carr]

Armorers loading .50 caliber ammo in the lethal end of the Lightning. [U.S. Air Force]

Stub Hatch in front of his aircraft. In an ill-conceived fighter attack on the oil fields at Ploesti, the 1st ran up a score of 29 enemy planes but lost 14 of its own ships - half of the force that went on the mission. Hatch became an ace by downing five ships himself. [H. Hatch]

Lightnings flying less than 50 feet from the ground through mountain passes of Yugoslavia at more than 200 miles per hour, often under sharp attack from light flak, missed their assigned target through navigational error and strafed a column of Red Army troops. Russian YAK fighters, protecting the column, attacked the US Lightnings and shot down two of them.

"Before the leaders of the groups of Allied fighters could establish recognition, two YAKS were shot down by US Lightnings. The Russian leader then courageously closed with the American leader and flew formation until identities were clearly confirmed and all fighters immediately broke off combat. Among those killed by the strafing was Russian Lt. General Kotov."

Lee K.Carr was on this mission and his is a slightly different version. "As we reached the valleys of mountainous Yugoslavia, Col. Edwinson sent the 97th Squadron down to strafe between Nic and Aleksinac. The remainder of the group continued on until we reached our target area. The 95th was on the deck with the 96th flying top cover. As we approached a small village we were certain we were where we were supposed to be. The 96th also confirmed this as we were on the deck while they were high enough to be able to see certain checkpoints. Right after we had hit a small train we spotted a troop column approaching the village. The column included troops and vehicles definitely looked to me like a retreating German column rather than an advancing Russian one. We did not see any markings of identification and there was no liaison between air and ground forces. Therefore we took for granted that this was the enemy. We had a field day in which a terrific amount of destruction was done. Many of the troops on the ground were killed including the Russian general.

Colonel O. B. Taylor's aircraft while commander of the 14th Fighter Group. The emblem on the engine nacelle was the group insignia - a black and silver shield with the motto "To Fight to Death" on a scroll below the shield. [O. Taylor]

The 459th was the only squadron to fly the Lightning in the Tenth Air Force. This ship belonged to William Broadfoot. [W. Broadfoot]

Another 459th ship was "Dixie Belle III"—a J-model flown by James Harris. The aircraft arrived in natural metal finish and were then painted in the field. Undersurfaces often came out a shade similar to duck egg green [with a more pronounced blue cast to it]. [W. Broadfoot]

As we started to pull up, a call came in that a bogie had shot down a P-38. A pilot from the 96th, without hesitation, jumped this bogie and blasted him from the sky. The rat race was on. Those who had just come up from strafing either were out of ammo or very low on it and I feel this saved many of the YAKS. The aerial combat continued with between five and seven of them going down in flames. Suddenly a call came over the radio: "I'm on the tail of one of the fighters. I'll check his tail markings. It's a red star! At this point Col. Edwinson's voice came through: It's the Russians - let's get the hell out of here!"

"Of the two P-38s lost in the action, one was shot down by the YAKS, but we really didn't know whether the other was lost to aircraft or ground fire. Lt. George Bowers got on the tail of one YAK during the fight and the Russian did his best to shake the Lightning. He did slow rolls and Bowers fired every time the Russian was at the bottom of the roll. Finally the YAK hit the deck and flew across a Russian airfield in the hope of having the Russian anti-aircraft shoot the P-38 off his tail. Bowers, seeing the planes on the ground beneath him dropped his nose and strafed the field. From what I saw that day, the YAK was no match at all for the Lightning."

After the 82nd landed back at Foggia, all hell broke loose. The brass came down to take each pilot's statement individually. The Russians wanted Curly Edwinson's scalp. In fact they wanted him shot. The Americans got him back to the States in a hurry to try and cool their Ally down. As a post script, it appears the 82nd did hit the right place after all. The Russians had made a major advance and had neglected to tell the Americans about it.

Above Burma and China

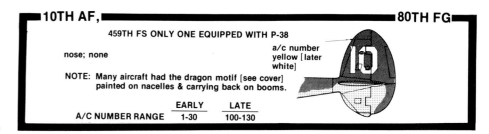

459TH FS ONLY ONE EQUIPPED WITH P-38

nose; none

a/c number
yellow [later white]

NOTE: Many aircraft had the dragon motif [see cover] painted on nacelles & carrying back on booms.

	EARLY	LATE
A/C NUMBER RANGE	1-30	100-130

Long before World War II began in Europe and other parts of the world, China and Japan were already involved in battle on the continent of Asia. Whenever the forces of the two countries met, the outcome was usually the same, the Chinese were defeated. Though the Chinese had an almost unlimited source of troops, they were poorly equipped and poorly led. The Japanese could defeat the forces in the field but they still faced the major problem of maintaining the lines of supply and communications over the vast distances in China. It was this rather than any army that kept the Japanese from total conquest of China.

The first American presence in the skies above China was the Flying Tigers and the fighter group it became (the 23rd) upon being absorbed into the USAAF. The tenth Air Force was the first American organization in the theater and controlled all U.S. air organizations until March 1943 when the Fourteenth Air Force was activated in China. After this, the Tenth handled the activities in Burma while the Fourteenth operated in China.

The story of the P-38 in the CBI actually had its start in the Mediterranean Theater in June 1943. On the ninth of the month a telegram arrived in Telergma stating that a P-38 project, complete with pilots and ground crew, would fly to China where the men would serve with the newly formed Fourteenth Air Force. Most of the personnel came from the three fighter groups operating in Africa. Some of the pilots were fresh from training but most had see action in the skies over North Africa. In mid-July, transports and fighters started the long trip eastward, first to India and then into China.

A flight of five P-38s buzzed low over the landing strip at Kunming, China on 25 July 1943 to mark the arrival of the type. Within hours of landing, a two ship flight was scrambled to intercept a Japanese raid. One of the Lightnings was shot down, the pilot bailing out safely, but Lt. Lowden Enslen was credited with the first enemy plane destroyed when he downed a ZERO.

Until 31 July, the P-38 Project still did not have an official designation. On that date, however, word came through that henceforth, it would be the 449th Fighter Squadron. The squadron was attached to the 23rd Fighter Group and on 14 August moved to its first permanent base at Lingling, China. In October, the squadron was reassigned—this time to the newly arrived 51st Fighter Group.

As was to be the case for the rest of the war, the 449th flew a wide variety of missions during its first several months of operations. The long range capability of the P-38 was put to use in escort missions to Hong Kong and other targets. Interception of incoming Japanese raids and bombing runs against targets in southeastern China were also called for.

On Thanksgiving day the pilots of the 449th were briefed to fly a mission to Formosa, the first time American planes would hit the island. Eight Lightnings were to spearhead a bomber attack on enemy airfields. As the aircraft roared over the Japanese field, it caught the troops on the ground by complete suprise. The normal day's operations were in progress with planes lined up along both sides. The Lightnings sped across the field with all guns blazing time after time. When the B-25s completed their bomb runs, the total destruction of between 50 and 60 planes was credited to the combined force. The 449th claimed ten of these. In the air, the squadron also scored well on the mission. Twelve Japanese planes were claimed with Captain Palmer getting three of these. Doubles were added by four other pilots.

February brought another change in station for the 449th. The new base was at Suichwan and it marked the most advanced airbase in the area. During and after the move, the 449th continued to fly a variety of missions. The Japanese raids on this field were more numerous and resulted in frequent combat. In May the Japanese launched a series of major attacks to try and knock the base out completely since an offensive was planned and Suichwan had to be neutralized. These were not successful and the Lightnings were able to fly a number of ground support sorties against the Japanese as they advanced.

The Chinese army was not able to stop the advance and by the middle of June it was obvious the squadron would have to evacuate Suichwan. The 449th continued to fly ground attack during the time the plans for the move were being made. On one of these, 24 June, Lt. Col. George McMillan, the squadron commander, was lost. Over a recently captured town, the Colonel's ship was riddled by ground fire. He was able to pull up and head for home but on the way, he had to make a forced landing. In the attempt, his ship crashed and McMillan was killed.

By mid-July, the squadron was at home in Chengkung in western China. Shortly after arriving, a flight of eight ships departed for Yunnanyi, an air base near the Burma border, where it remained to support the Allied drive across northern Burma. On 29 July, another flight left for a staging field in southeastern China. Here they refueled and joined forces with a large number of B-24s for an attack on Hainan Island. Flying top cover for the bombers, thirteen Lightnings were intercepted by a force of 25 Japaneses planes. In the fight which followed, the P-38s ran up a score of seven victories. In the year of action since the first fight, these victories brought the total for the squadron to 74 with another 21 probably destroyed and 25 damaged.

In the Tenth Air Force, one squadron of Lightnings also served in action to drive the Japanese back from the border of India and then out of Burma. The 459th Fighter Squadron was activated on 1 September 1943 as a fourth squadron to the 80th Fighter Group. Pilots and ground personnel came from the 80th, 311th and from Operational Training Units in the Theater. The 459th was to be a twin-engine squadron but initially it flew P-40s. By November, the unit was pronounced ready for combat and, on 20 November, flew its first mission.

The squadron, as did all fighter groups in the Burma-India Theater, flew a

H. H. Sealy in front of "Haleakala" named for the Hawaiian fire god. During the period when this photo was taken, most of the ships in the squadron carried variations on the dragon motif. Also, the ten victories displayed include both air and ground kills. [W. Broadfoot]

different type of mission almost every day. Japanese supply and communications centers were frequent targets. Escort missions and dive-bombing attacks were also flown. The first victories came on 9 December when Hampton Boggs and W.R. Thompson each downed an enemy fighter. After a big raid on airfields near Maymyo, Burma on 26 December, the squadron saw little action for the next three months. During this period, the pilots went to gunnery school and then moved to a new base—Chittagong—near the Bay of Bengal and Burma. This put the Lightnings much closer to the enemy and marked the beginning of a high scoring period.

From 11 March to 26 May the 459th flew a total of 58 combat days & destroyed a total of 128 Japanese planes including some 60 in the air. A goal

had been set to drive the enemy from the air over Burma and the squadron certainly did its share. So fierce was the air war in March that the Japanese were forced to cease operations from their bases close to the fighting in northern Burma. To support their troops, aircraft had to fly all the way from Rangoon—a distance of some 600 miles.

The heavy action opened on 11 March. As the squadron war diary puts it: "Surprising the Japanese over Aungban at 0800 hours this morning, Captain Luering led his twelve Lightnings in just as the enemy fighters were taking off to intercept. The unfortunate Japanese were hardly off the ground as the Lightnings swept in and picked them off one by one as they attempted to gain altitude. With burning wrecks dotting the countryside, Captain Luehring pressed home the advantage of terrific airspeed, accumulated in the downward glide from Aunguan, and, zooming the 38s high above the remaining airborne enemy, made another pass and swept the air clean." In this action, twelve Japanese planes were shot down and another seven destroyed on the ground.

Though the 459th was attached to the 80th Fighter Group, in reality, it operated pretty much on its own. On 13 March, it was divorced from the group that had given it birth. The 459th then operated under the administrative control of Tenth Air Force and the tactical control of the British Third Tactical Air Force. The move seemed to give the men a lift and a greater sense of its own identity.

Until the monsoon season opened and curtailed operations, the Lightnings kept up the series of raids on Japanese air fields in central Burma. The enemy airmen were becoming all too aware of the P-38 as evidenced by the following excerpt from one of the 459th pilot's report of a mission: "I made a pass on Heho (a Japanese airfield) from 10,000 feet and opened fire on a taxiing Oscar. The pilot, in a black suit, jumped out of the moving plane and fell to the ground. The Oscar continued on its own and rolled off the runway."

The last big fight before the monsoons came on the same day the Allies stormed ashore on the beaches of Normandy—6 June. Eighteen Lightnings left on another mission to Heho. One of the men along was Billy Broadfoot and he remembers: "We got jumped at the western edge of Burma Valley when we were about out of gas and ammo. It was a hellava fight and we lost Lt. Goodrich but did knock down two Japanese planes and damaged a bunch more. As we were heading for home, Captain Walter F. Duke, the top ace in the Tenth Air Force, couldn't contact his wingman and radioed us he was going to make one more circle to look for him. We never saw Duke again but his wingman did make it back to base. After the war Hampton Boggs was assigned a DC-3 and an interpreter to go all over the Japanese bases in Burma and interogate their intelligence officers. He found that the day Duke was lost, a flight of Japanese fighters had remained up high and out of the fight. When we went away and Duke was alone, they jumped him from above. The Japs confirmed that he had shot down three of them before they finally got him." Duke was officially credited with ten aerial victories but these three would make his unofficial score thirteen.

Missions were still flown during the summer of 1944 but there was virtually no aerial combat. Also the weather was bad and this severely limited the ability to fly. The air war in Burma had been won—the 459th scored only ten more victories after 6 June—but there was still the important job of ground support. These missions were important for they did provide an easier path for the ground troops to tread.

Pacific Lightnings Part II

The formation of the Far East Air Force on 15 June 1943 was a move to consolidate American air power in the Pacific for the upcoming invasion of the Philippines. The bases available for the FEAF were still too far from many of the targets of interest to allow fighter escort. Consequently, Noemfoor and finally Cape Sansapor, on the western tip of New Guinea, were taken by the end of July and work readying bases at these locations began almost immediately. Air opposition to the Americans had virtually ceased over New Guinea by the end of June and most missions flown by the Lightnings were of a ground support nature.

Even with advanced bases, there was still a need to increase the range of the fighters. Fortunately, an expert on long distance flight, Charles A. Lindbergh, had shown up on New Guinea completely unannounced. At first the brass was not exactly sure how to handle their guest, but General Kenney requested he be allowed to stay in the area and teach long distance flying techniques to the P-38 pilots. Lindbergh agreed and went to the home of the 475th Fighter Group, Hollandia, to start his teaching.

The 475th, as with the other units, felt that a six and a half to seven hour mission was really stretching the Lightning to its limit. After some due consideration, Lindbergh announced his solution at a special pilot's meeting in early July: "Now if you fly at 1,600 rpm with sufficient manifold pressure to maintain a slow cruise speed, you should be able to stay out nine hours easily. Of course, it will be necessary for you to lean your mixture controls as far back as possible. By carefully using your throttles and low rpm, I can see no reason why you should not also have the capability of fighting five or ten minutes over a distant target."

Lindbergh wanted to go along on some of the missions to see how well the men had learned their lessons. General Kenney could understand his feelings, but as he was a civilian and a famous person, he could also see the serious repercussions if Lindbergh should be shot down. Since, New Guinea was clear of enemy aircraft, however, Kenney did authorize Lindbergh to go on a few missions in this area. Lindbergh stretched this a bit on one mission and went along on a mission to Ceram. A lone Japanese aircraft was encountered and Lindbergh shot it down. To avoid any problems, no request for credit was requested by Lindbergh and this victory does not show up on 475th Fighter

[Top] In July 1944, Charles Lindbergh spent a good bit of time with the pilots of the 475th teaching them new techniques to extend the range of their fighters. He is seen here talking to Tommy McGuire. [J. Loisel]

[Left] Filling the external tanks. [80th Fighter Squadron Assoc.]

[Right] P-38J-15-LO in flight. [W. Hess]

"Miss Ruby Louise" of the 80th Fighter Squadron is the plane closest to the camera. [80th Fighter Squadron Association]

Engineering area of the 432nd Fighter Squadron on Mindoro. The tip of the tails and the rear half of the spinner are in yellow. [J. Loisel]

Group records. Shortly after this mission, Lindbergh was almost shot down and General Kenney suggested, in rather strong terms, it would be a good idea if Lindbergh would wrap up his activities and head for home. He did, but he left a legacy with the P-38 pilots in the FEAF - the ability to increase range by almost 50 percent.

The 1st of September was a milestone in the history of the Fifth Air Force for on that day, B-24s carried out the first daylight mission over the Philippines since early 1942. No fighters went along on this strike at Davao, but on the next mission, fifty P-38s did go as escort. General Barnes of the Thirteenth requested that a few of the Lightnings be allowed to go on the mission to practice the new long range techniques. This request was granted and six P-38s from the Thirteenth went along. Three Japanese fighters came up to intercept the formation—all were knocked down quickly. Much to the annoyance of the pilots from the Fifth, one of the victories was scored by a jockey from the Thirteenth.

Balikpapan, on the coast of Borneo, was the center of an extremely rich petroleum field. Refineries in the area produced much of the aviation fuel required to keep Japanese planes in the air. Until the American bases on the western end of New Guinea were operational, this vital target was beyond the reach of the American B-24s. By the end of September, however, everything was ready to go. On the 30th, 72 bombers, without fighter escort set out for Balikpapan. Enemy fighters rose in strength and knocked four of the bombers down. This was almost ten percent of the bombers that actually made the complete mission (26 B-24s turned back with a variety of problems). On 3 October, another strike was launched, but the Japanese were really ready for them and the 307th Bomb Group lost seven of the twenty planes it put over the

target. These losses could not be tolerated, but Balikpapan had to be knocked from the war.

Fighter escort had to be provided if the operations against Balikpapan were to continue. There was a problem—it was 830 miles to the target and even with the new long range techniques, it would be difficult. After much calculation, the planners of the FEAF determined the fighters could make the trip and on 10 October, a major attack was launched. A total of 106 B-24s with an escort of P-47s sweeping ahead and P-38s protecting above swept in. Four bombers were lost but a number of Japanese fighters were downed. Four days later another major strike was launched with even better results. One more bombing mission was flown, but by then the attention of the FEAF was shifted to the Philippines.

After Dick Bong had destroyed his 28th aircraft in April, he had been sent back to the States on a goodwill trip. While there he also finally had the chance to go to gunnery school. Upon his return to the Fifth Air Force, General Kenney put him on his staff to go to the individual fighter units and teach the pilots what he had learned. Though he was discouraged from going on combat missions, he was able to get half-hearted permission when he argued that the only way to determine whether the lessons were being learned was to see his pupils in action.

The first combat mission he flew after his return was the 10 October flight to Balikpapan. He went along with his old comrades in the 9th Fighter Squadron and came away with two victories. When questioned by General Kenney, Bong assured the General that he had been along as an instructor and he had to shoot the two planes strictly in self defense. Kenney remarked that the gunnery training must have done him some good. To this, Bong replied:

80th Fighter Squadron ships taxiing out for takeoff. [80th Fighter Squadron Association]

Late markings of the 80th included green on the top and bottom portions of the tail. [80th Fighter Squadron Association]

"General, it really was a good course, but just to make sure, I pushed the gun barrels into the other guy's cockpit and then pulled the trigger."

On the morning of 20 October 1944, American troops came ashore on the island of Leyte. After an absense of well over two years, McArthur had returned to the Philippines. The Japanese were taken by surprise but it wasn't long before they responded in force. On 24-25 October the decisive Battle of Leyte Gulf was faught with the virtual destruction of the Japanese fleet. Air support for the invasion and in the few first days ashore was provided by Navy aircraft flying off the American carriers. It was mandatory, however, that facilities be established rapidly so that the land based fighters of the FEAF could operate. Airfields were captured at Tacloban and Dulag on the first two days of the invasion, and crews were put to work readying these to take aircraft. On the morning of 27 October the last section of pierced steel planking was laid at Tacloban and shortly after 34 Lightnings of the 7th and 9th Fighter Squadrons (all three squadrons of the 49th Fighter Group had been equipped with the fighter since September) came in for a landing.

The 8th Fighter Group was still back on Morotai at the end of October. On the 30th, the 36th Squadron, under the leadership of W.K. "Kenny" Giroux, flew a strike against the airfield at Sandakan on the northern tip of Borneo. The eleven ship formation strafed the airfield where six Japanese were destroyed. Giroux then led his formation in an attack on two tankers in a nearby harbor. Down he went on a strafing pass at deck level. The ship threw up a shower of anti-aircraft fire but the American pilot held his course. He opened fire and just as he pulled up over the ship a violent explosion buffeted his plane—his shots had hit a depth charge and the whole ship had gone up underneath him. After he passed over the ship and found his Lightning would still fly, Giroux looked

back to see the tanker broken in half and starting to sink. The squadron made several passes at the second tanker and left it burning badly and listing.

The sinking of the ship was the start of a remarkable week for Giroux. On 2 November, while escorting B-24s over Negros Island, he shot down three Oscars. Two days later he added another triple to bring his score to one ship and six aircraft.

November marked a two month shooting spree for all the P-38 units in the Fifth. The Japanese had been holding air strength in the Philippines against the day the Americans actually landed & now that they were ashore, the Japanese threw everything they had at US positions. Big air battles developed virtually every mission. On 2 November, the 49th blasted 26 aircraft from the sky. The 475th entered claims for 70 aircraft in November and over 90 the following month. The aces who were still active added to their scores and many pilots who had not even seen a Japanese plane before, joined the ranks of these who had downed five or more enemy aircraft.

The two groups of Thirteenth Air Force Lightnings did not get in on the early action around Leyte but these units also added to their scores. Strikes against Japanese bases in the central Philippines and in the Celebes were among the principal targets. On 1 November a strike on Cebu resulted in claims for a number of aircraft including three by the leading ace of the Thriteenth Air Force, Lt. Colonel Robert B. Westbrook. Ten days later, another Thirteenth pilot, Don S. Warner, downed three Zeros in a battle again over Cebu.

December was a period when both Dick Bong and Tommy McGuire continued to add to their scores. At the beginning of the month these two stood one-two in terms of aerial victories. A strong rivalry had developed

Under leaden skies, a Lightning starts its roll for take off. [W. Hess]

Captain Chris Herman of the 475th Fighter Group. At this time, the 431st Squadron painted the red devil emblem, its symbol, on the radiator housings of many of its ships. [Air Force Museum]

The final scoreboard painted on Tommy McGuire's plane. McGuire wanted desperately to pass Dick Bong's 40 victories [note the space for four more victories]. [Air Force Museum]

between the two pilots but several times this month, they flew on the same mission and in the same flight.

Both the Americans and the Japanese decided to land troops on the western side of Leyte on 7 December. Vicious fighting, in the air and on the ground, occurred as the two forces struggled to determine which one would remain. In the morning, McGuire flew one mission on which he downed an Oscar. That same afternoon he went on another with Dick Bong as his element lead. Shortly after arriving in the area, Bong called in a bogey and promptly dispatched it. A little later he added a Tojo to his score, now at 38, when the two planes came at one another in a head on pass. McGuire also ran his score to 30 when he downed a Tojo.

McGuire shot down a Jack on the 13th and, on the 15th Bong kept his lead over the 475th Fighter Group pilot by blasting an Oscar. The 17th again found Bong flying with McGuire and the 431st. Each downed an Oscar to run their scores to 40 and 32 respectively. After this mission, General Kenney grounded Bong. With forty victories to his credit, he was slated to return to the States for another publicity campaign. He argued against this as he wanted to try for 50, but the general was adamant. Before he left for the United States, however, Richard Bong was presented with the Congressional Medal of Honor for his actions during his second tour of duty.

In the two day period of 25-26 December, Tommy McGuire added six victories to his total. Two of these came as a Christmas present while the other four, all Zekes, were scored the next day. This brought his total score to 38, only two behind the now departed Dick Bong. From the time McGuire started

scoring he had remained eight behind. Even when Bong returned to the States the first time, McGuire didn't have a chance to close the gap—he was grounded with malaria. Now the victory leadership was in sight. When he landed, however, he was told he was temporarily grounded. Bong was on his way back to the States with a big welcome scheduled and General Kenney did not want him to arrive and find he was the second leading scorer. The general told McGuire he could go back on operations after Bong had received the welcome prepared for him.

The 30th of December brought the last wartime victory for the 80th Fighter Squadron. Captain Louis Schriber led a patrol to the San Jose Valley, but he was forced to abort the mission and return to base. Shortly after, bogies were reported in the area and Schriber took another Lightning up to intercept. After joining a flight already in the air, he spotted four bombers flying on the deck and went down to attack. He caught the tail end aircraft in the formation and fired several long bursts. The Japanese plane broke in two in front of the tail and crashed into a river bed. Schriber also entered claims for a probable and a damaged on this mission.

January found Tommy McGuire back in the air and looking for the victories he needed to pass Bong's score. With Major Jack Rittmayer (four victories), Captain Edwin Weaver, and Lieutenant Douglas Thropp (one victory) as the other members, he took off on the morning of 7 January 1945 to fly a sweep to Negros Island. The flight didn't find any action over the first air field it tried and headed off to look for the enemy elsewhere. A few minutes later an enemy aircraft was spotted coming in from dead ahead, but before any one could fire,

Jay T. Robbins in front of "Jandina IV". Robbins was the top ace of the 8th Fighter Group with 22 victories to his credit. [80th Fighter Squadron Assoc.]

[Top Left] The end of the war found the 80th Fighter Squadron on the island of le Shima, Just off the coast of Okinawa. The figure on the nacelle is the emblem of the squadron—a head-hunter. [80th Fighter Squadron Association]

For a period, aircraft of the 36th Fighter Squadron carried numbers rather than individual aircraft numbers. This ship, flown by Kenny Giroux, had its intakes as well as portions of the spinners in black.

it passed beneath the formation then wheeled around on the tail of the Americans and opened fire on Thropp. The aircraft, originally identified as a Zeke but since determined to be an Oscar flown by Warrant Officer Akira Sugimoto, was on the inside of a very tight turn at 300 feet. Rittmayer fired a burst at the Japanese plane and forced him to break off the pass by tightening his turn. Now Weaver's ship came in the line of fire. McGuire was slightly above and tried to tighten his turn, but his aircraft stalled out. McGuire's ship snap-rolled to the left until it was in an inverted position with the nose down about 30 degrees. In this position it slammed into the ground and exploded.

[Top] The men of the 80th pose before "S". Of special note are the spinners and wing bands in green. [80th Fighter Squadron Association]

[Right]Camouflaged aircraft remained in service for long after most ships were flying in natural metal garb. Of special interest is the aircraft letter which appears to be yellow. [80th Fighter Squadron Association]

Tommy McGuire, the second leading American ace of all time was dead.

The three remaining American planes were not through with action yet. The Oscar disappeared in to the overcast but soon another plane came at the Lightnings. Though the pilots thought this was the same aircraft, it was a Frank flown by Sgt. Mizunori Fekuda. With his first burst, he hit Thropp's left engine and then swung around for another pass. It was only now the P-38s dropped the auxiliary tanks they had been carrying. Again, Fekuda opened fire with deadly accuracy. Rittmayer's ship was hit and crashed. What had started as a fighter sweep had ended with two US pilots dead and a third with a crippled aircraft. For his excellent combat record, McGuire received the Congressional Medal of Honor.

Four days later tragedy again struck a top ace. Lt. Colonel Robert Westbrook, the top gun in the Thirteenth Air Force was killed. On a strafing mission against Japanese shipping, Westbrook and his wingman zeroed in on an enemy gunboat while the rest of the flight went after some cargo vessels. In the attack both were shot down. The wingman was rescued by a PBY but no trace was found of Westbrook.

The level of quality of the Japanese fighter pilot had dropped off by this stage in the war. The air war in New Guinea and then over the Philippines had stripped the Empire of many of its better pilots. There were, however, still some of the really good ones around. John Loisel, who joined the 475th when it was being formed and later rose to command the unit, remembered an engagement in April 1945: "My last air-to-air combat came over Nha Trang, Indo China. I was leading the mission and jumped a formation of Japanese fighters covering a Japanese Convoy of ships. On the first pass, I shot down one of the Franks, and then tried to nail the leader. With several flights following—possessing every advantage in the books—I chased him to the deck and unsuccessfully pursued him for a good fifteen minutes. I didn't even put a hole in him. I finally had to call it off and head for Clark because of fuel. While trying to get this one lone plane who had shot down one of our P-38s on the initial contact, I tried every trick I knew. (Loisel ended up with eleven victories so he did know a few.) The fact that he could out maneuver several flights of P-38s tells something."

During the summer of 1945, the American fighter forces moved to bases near Okinawa. From here the Japanese homeland was within easy reach of the aircraft of the FEAF. It would be the jumping-off point for the aerial prelude to the planned invasion of Japan.

On 14 August, five P-38s of the 35th Fighter Squadron flew an escort mission for two rescue planes. Near Japan, six Franks were spotted and the P-38 pilots dove to attack them. Raymond Meyer blasted two ships while his mates, George Stevens, Billy Moore and Dwight Hollister added single victories each. These were the last aerial victories scored by Fifth Air Force fighters. The next day the war was over.

P-38L-5-LOs of a U.S. based training unit in formation. Note how the engine exhaust has all but obliterated the serial number on the planes. [W. Hess]

[Right] P-38J-15-LO fresh from the factory. [W. Hess]